Economic Freedom of the States of India 2013

Friedrich Naumann STIFTUNG FÜR DIE FREIHEIT | CATO INSTITUTE | INDICUS ANALYTICS

Authors

Bibek Debroy is Professor, Centre for Policy Research, Delhi. He is an economist and has worked in academic institutes and for the government. His primary research interests are education, health, law, governance and trade. He is the author of several books, papers and popular articles.

Laveesh Bhandari, recipient of best thesis award by the EXIM Bank of India in 1996, and Hite Fellowship for work in International Finance. His areas of work are macro- economic research, large-frame surveys on economic and social sectors and consumer profiles, policy analysis, econometric modelling, monitoring and evaluation. His work on inequality, education and India's progress is frequently referred to in the policy debate in India. He has authored and co-authored numerous publications on socioeconomic development, health, education, poverty and inequality.

Swaminathan S. Anklesaria Aiyar is a research fellow at the Cato Institute with a special focus on India and Asia. His research interests include economic change in developing countries, human rights and civil strife, political economy, energy, trade and industry. He is a prolific columnist and TV commentator in India, well-known for a popular weekly column titled "Swaminomics" in the Times of India. He is the author of Escape from the Benevolent Zookeepers: The Best of Swaminomics (New Delhi: Times of India, 2008) and has been called "India's leading economic journalist" by Stephen Cohen of the Brookings Institution. He has been the editor of India's two biggest financial dailies, The Economic Times and Financial Express, and was also the India correspondent of The Economist for two decades. He has frequently been a consultant to the World Bank and Asian Development Bank. Currently, he is consulting editor of The Economic Times. Swami spends part of the year in India and part in the USA. He holds a Master's degree in economics from Oxford University, UK.

Economic Freedom of the States of India 2013

Bibek Debroy
Laveesh Bhandari
Swaminathan S. Anklesaria Aiyar

ACADEMIC FOUNDATION
NEW DELHI

www.academicfoundation.com

First published in 2014 by

ACADEMIC FOUNDATION
47/2-73 / 23 Bharat Ram Road, (23 Ansari Road),
Darya Ganj, New Delhi - 110 002 (India).
Phones : 23245001 / 02 / 03 / 04.
Fax : +91-11-23245005.
E-mail : books@academicfoundation.com
www.academicfoundation.com

Published in association with :

FRIEDRICH-NAUMANN-STIFTUNG FÜR DIE FREIHEIT
www.southasia.fnst.org

in partnership with :

CATO INSTITUTE
www.cato.org

INDICUS ANALYTICS
www.indicus.net

Cataloging in Publication Data--DK

Courtesy: D.K. Agencies (P) Ltd. <docinfo@dkagencies.com>

Debroy, Bibek.
Economic freedom of the states of India, 2013 / Bibek Debroy, Laveesh Bhandari, Swaminathan S. Anklesaria Aiyar.

p. cm.

ISBN 9789332701359

1. Economic development--India. 2. India--Economic policy--1991- 3. Agriculture and state--India. 4. Manpower policy--India. 5. Free enterprise--India. 6. Economic surveys--India. I. Bhandari, Laveesh, joint author. II. Aiyar, Swaminathan S. Anklesaria, joint author. III. Title.

DDC 338.954 23

Typeset by Italics India, New Delhi.

Printed and bound by The Book Mint, New Delhi.
www.thebookmint.in

Contents

List of Tables

Foreword

The *Economic Freedom of the World* (EFW) project begun in the 1980s by the Fraser Institute shows an enduring empirical relationship between economic freedom and prosperity, growth and improvements in human well-being. This study grows out of that work and seeks to measure the level of economic freedom within vast, diverse India.

While the economic freedom of India has notably increased since the introduction of market reforms in the early 1990s—a period that has also seen improvements in the country's indicators of human development—India's ratings remain low on the global index and have fallen somewhat in recent years. This year's report highlights the importance of state-level policy improvements and experimentation to produce better economic and social outcomes, especially in light of the national government's lack of interest or ability to continue reforms. Although the median economic freedom rating of the states of India has increased since 2005, the levels of economic freedom within the country vary greatly, with numerous states showing significant increases or significant declines in their ratings.

A chapter by Swaminathan Aiyar focuses on Bihar, the state with the lowest economic freedom rating that has nevertheless managed a remarkable improvement in its economic and social performance. Starting from a very low base, Bihar increased its economic freedom rating by a proportionately greater degree than the increase in the national average. It did so by, among other things, providing badly lacking public security. The resulting increase in growth and large fall in poverty were helped by the more liberal national policy environment set forth in the 1990s, showing that states can take advantage of the progress begun by the national government. Another chapter by Bibek Debroy meticulously enumerates how centralisation at the national level violates the Constitution and constrains the economic freedom of the states.

The Cato Institute is pleased once again to co-publish the annual *Economic Freedom of the States of India* (EFSI) report with the Friedrich Naumann Foundation and Indicus Analytics. We hope it will serve policy makers and interested laypersons as a guide to better policies.

— Ian Vásquez
Director,
Center for Global Liberty and Prosperity,
Cato Institute

The *Economic Freedom of the States of India* (EFSI), 2013 report brings out once again the significant differences in economic governance between the states of India. It thus has focused attention on state-level reforms to improve inclusive economic growth. The Index is based on the Fraser Institute's *Economic Freedom of the World* (EFW) report. This was developed on the basis of ideas of Milton Friedman, Charles Buchanan, Douglass North, Michael Walker and others who wanted an empirically sound way to measure whether economic freedom would lead to better economic and social outcomes. This is indeed the case, as the annual study has clearly demonstrated, and the index has become an important contribution to the international policy debate. Its success has inspired researchers to come up with sub-national indices to capture the performance of sub-national institutions in China, Germany and elsewhere. The Friedrich-Naumann-Stiftung has been supporting the development of an Economic Freedom Index for the states of India for several years now. This index has become an important part of India's reform discourse.

The Indian Index is based on the three parameters: size of the government; legal structure and security of property rights; and regulation of business and labour. The Indian Index ranks 20 states of India for which data is available. The researchers have used published data from official sources or reputed institutions to produce the Index.

The researchers producing the Index are distinguished economists from India. Bibek Debroy and Laveesh Bhandari are known for their work in suggesting policy recommendations for Indian economic growth. The Cato Institute, a prominent and leading American think-tank based in Washington, DC, has been a partner in this endeavour for several years now. Swaminathan S. Anklesaria Aiyar, a well-known writer and commentator, is the third co-author representing Cato.

The Index shows the direct correlation between economic freedom and the well-being of citizens. As the World Index has shown a direct correlation between economic freedom and national indicators of human and material progress, the same correlation is also visible at the sub-national level. States in India which are economically more free are also doing better in terms of a higher per capita growth for its citizens, unemployment levels are lower in these states, sanitary conditions are better and the states also attract more investments.

Each report shines a spotlight on a different state. The current report focuses on Bihar, a place traditionally at the bottom of the table with regard to most indicators but a state that has seen some major reforms pushed by the state government. The question is if and to what extent these reforms have made a dent in Bihar's ranking.

Another focus in the current report is the changing relations between the central government and the states in India. The big question is whether more decentralisation will lead to more creative and successful policy reform

The report is published through a joint effort of the Friedrich-Naumann-Stiftung für die Freiheit, the Cato Institute and the Academic Foundation, New Delhi. We would like to thank all the contributors, authors and partners for their enthusiasm and hard work that made this report possible. May it prove to be a useful instrument for research and debate for policymakers and academics alike.

— Siegfried Herzog
Regional Director, South Asia,
Friedrich-Naumann-Stiftung für die Freiheit

Executive Summary

The *Economic Freedom of the States of India* (EFSI), 2013, estimates economic freedom in the 20 biggest Indian states, based to the extent possible on data for 2012, using a methodology adapted from the Fraser Institute's *Economic Freedom of the World* (EFW) annual reports. The main highlights of our report this year are as follows:

1. Gujarat has widened its lead at the top of the economic freedom table, with an index score of 0.65 (on a scale from 0 to 1.0). Tamil Nadu remains in second position, but some distance behind, with a score of 0.54. Next in line come Andhra Pradesh (0.50), Haryana (0.49), Himachal Pradesh (0.47) and Madhya Pradesh (0.47) (see Table 0.1).

2. Overall, the states have become freer over time. The median score for economic freedom among states had earlier declined from 0.38 in 2005 to 0.36 in 2009, but has now improved to 0.43. However, this is way behind the top score of 0.65 registered by Gujarat, showing that most states have a long way to go yet.

Table 0.1

Economic Freedom of the States: Index Scores and Rankings, 2005 and 2013

	Rank		*Score*	
	2013	2005	2013	2005
Gujarat	1	5	0.65	0.46
Tamil Nadu	2	1	0.54	0.57
Andhra Pradesh	3	7	0.50	0.40
Haryana	4	4	0.49	0.47
Himachal Pradesh	5	3	0.47	0.48
Madhya Pradesh	6	2	0.47	0.49
Rajasthan	7	12	0.46	0.37
Chhattisgarh	8	16	0.44	0.33
Karnataka	9	13	0.43	0.36
Kerala	10	10	0.42	0.38
Maharashtra	11	9	0.42	0.40
Jammu & Kashmir	12	15	0.41	0.34
Punjab	13	6	0.40	0.41
Uttarakhand	14	17	0.39	0.33
Odisha	15	11	0.36	0.37
Uttar Pradesh	16	14	0.36	0.35
West Bengal	17	18	0.35	0.31
Jharkhand	18	8	0.33	0.40
Assam	19	19	0.32	0.30
Bihar	20	20	0.31	0.25

3. The three states recording the fastest improvement in economic freedom have been among the fastest-growing states. Growth has averaged 10.1 per cent in Gujarat, 8.5 per cent in Chhattisgarh and 8.8 per cent in Andhra Pradesh (see Table 1.8).

4. Gujarat is not only the freest state, but it has also registered the fastest rate of improvement (from 0.46 to 0.65). The second fastest improver is Andhra Pradesh (from 0.40 to 0.50).

5. The bottom three states, in reverse order, are Bihar (0.31), Assam (0.32) and Jharkhand (0.33). Bihar has long been last in this league and continues to be last despite significant improvement after Nitish Kumar became Chief Minister in 2005. Assam remains at 19th position. Jharkhand has worsened more than any other state, with its index score falling from 0.40 in 2005 to 0.33 in 2013. Because of this, it has slipped from 8th position to 18th. It has also recorded one of the lowest rates of economic growth (7.0%). Jharkhand claims that it has been held back by Maoist insurrection in several districts, but this is a weak excuse for poor governance. Assam and Jammu & Kashmir have been other relatively slow-growing states (see Table 1.8).

6. The biggest improvement has been recorded by Chhattisgarh, which has moved up from 16th to 8th position. This state has an even worse problem of Maoism than Jharkhand, but has shown that improved governance and rapid gross domestic product (GDP) growth are nevertheless possible in such difficult circumstances. Rajasthan is another state that has shown much improvement, moving up from 12th to 7th position. On the other hand, Punjab's rank has slipped substantially, from 6th to 13th position. Its score has remained almost unchanged, but many other states have improved their scores while Punjab has not.

7. This report has a special chapter on the remarkable improvement in Bihar's economic and social performance in the last decade. Bihar's freedom index score has improved significantly from 0.25 in 2005 to 0.31 in 2013. But it remains in last position among the 20 states because its starting point was so far behind the others. Under Chief Minister Nitish Kumar, its GDP growth rate averaged 11.8 per cent between 2004-05 and 2010-11. It used to be the poorest state but slashed its poverty headcount ratio from 56 per cent in 2009-2011 to just 33.74 per cent in 2011-12, and is no longer the poorest. Its overall literacy rate improved by 16.8 percentage points and its female literacy rate by 20 percentage points in the decade 2001-2011 (the highest among states in both cases). The main pillars of Nitish Kumar's strategy were the improved provision of two essential government services (technically called public goods) needed for the proper functioning of the state—public order and

good road connectivity. By putting almost 80,000 top gangsters in jail, he ended the earlier 'jungle raj' (rule of the jungle), created safety and personal security for citizens, and hence made it safe for entrepreneurs to invest in and expand businesses. His massive road-building programme brought connectivity and economic opportunity to areas lacking both. He was helped greatly by national economic reforms starting in 1991 that created a liberal economic climate that backward states like Bihar were able to take advantage of. Rapid economic development helped Kumar tackle the menace of Maoism, with violent incidents down from 1,309 in 2001-2005 to 514 in 2006-2010, and civilian deaths down from 760 to 214.

8. The improvement in Bihar's economic freedom score, from 0.25 in 2005 to 0.31 in 2013, is significant but not spectacular. Yet, starting from a very low base, it represents an improvement of one-fourth, much better than the national average improvement of one-tenth. Many but not all of Bihar's individual freedom indicators have improved. The recovery of stolen property remains dismally low; judicial vacancies have worsened even as the national rate has improved; and the proportion of violent crime, though falling, is almost double the national average. Almost half the legislators from Nitish Kumar's own party face criminal charges. In neighbouring Odisha, Chief Minister Naveen Patnaik has sacked many of his ministers for corruption. But Kumar has not done the same in Bihar, although corruption is widely regarded as very high. So, while the quality of governance has improved a lot in Bihar, it is still unsatisfactory.

9. This report has a special chapter on centre-state relations, making the point that the economic freedom of the states is constrained by excessive centralisation of economic power. This centralisation also violates the spirit of the Constitution, and needs dilution. For instance, states cannot borrow except with Reserve Bank of India (RBI) permission. Discretionary flows of funds through the Planning Commission to the states must be reduced, by drastically pruning the current 200 odd centrally sponsored schemes (CSS). The Finance Commission currently recommends a formula periodically for sharing tax revenue between the centre and states. But its formula does not apply to borrowed central funds used for investment (plan spending), whose distribution is decided arbitrarily by New Delhi. The distinction between Plan and non-Plan spending is arbitrary and hurts an integrated view of development, in which maintenance spending is as important as Plan spending. The Finance Commission formula is supposed to help backward states improve their public services to a minimum standard, but in practice it is deficient.

1

The State of Economic Freedom in India 2013

Bibek Debroy and Laveesh Bhandari

Background

Man is born free, but is everywhere in chains, said Jean-Jacques Rousseau. This report is based on the philosophy that freedom is both precious in itself and a path to prosperity. It is the latest in our series of reports measuring economic freedom in different states of India. *Economic Freedom of the States of India* (EFSI), 2013, uses data relating to 2012.

Economic freedom isn't the only kind of freedom: political liberties and civil rights are also aspects of freedom. Unlike some other studies, this report seeks to measure economic freedom alone. It draws on and adapts a methodology already established in *Economic Freedom of the World* (EFW), an annual publication of the Fraser Institute (co-published in the United States by the Cato Institute), that has been brought out since 1996. This is in line with the methodology used in our reports for earlier years. The full details of the methodology are given in the Appendix II.

Table 1.1 shows how India scores in the *EFW 2013* report, based on data up to 2011. Economic freedom in India rose from an index score of just 5.15 in 1980 to a peak of 6.72 in 2005 (on a scale from 1 to 10), but then declined a bit to 6.24 in 2010, before recovering marginally to 6.34 in 2011. India ranks only 111th out of 152 countries in the EFW list, having slipped from 76th position in 2005. Clearly its government has attached a low priority to improving economic freedom.

Of the five parameters making up the EFW scores, India has seen dramatic improvement only in one—freedom to trade internationally—where the score has gone up from 3.00 in 1980 to 6.26 in 2011. In regulation of credit, labour and business, its score has improved more slowly but steadily, from 5.68 to 6.76. In other parameters, India has fallen from peaks achieved earlier. In size of government, it is down to 6.35 from a peak of 7.42 in 2005; in legal structure and security of property rights, it is down to 5.68 from a peak of 6.51 in 2005; and in access to sound money, it is down to 6.67 from a peak of 6.88 in 2000. Despite this lack of clear commitment to economic

Table 1.1

India's Scores in Economic Freedom of the World

	1980	1985	1990	1995	2000	2005	2009	2010	2011
Summary rating	5.15	4.83	4.89	5.76	6.32	6.72	6.31	6.24	6.34
Size of the government	5.00	4.50	4.88	6.26	6.83	7.42	6.33	6.37	6.35
Legal structure and security of property rights	5.78	4.92	4.39	5.87	5.99	6.51	5.78	5.55	5.68
Access to sound money	6.29	6.61	6.63	6.50	6.88	6.84	6.55	6.42	6.67
Freedom to trade internationally	3.00	2.40	2.67	4.50	5.51	6.07	6.20	6.28	6.26
Regulation of credit, labour and business	5.68	5.70	5.87	5.66	6.40	6.74	6.68	6.70	6.76

Source: Economic Freedom of the World 2013 (unadjusted series), p.89.

freedom, India's economic performance was very good between 2003 and 2010, but has decelerated sharply since. India's GDP growth was 9.2 per cent in 2010-11 but has more than halved to just 4.4 per cent in the second quarter of 2013, and its GDP in the full fiscal year will probably be well below 5 per cent. There are many reasons for this deceleration, but one of them must be the decline in economic freedom.

The good news is that economic freedom in the states of India has improved even as it has decreased in India as a whole. In other words, state capitals have done more to improve economic freedom than New Delhi has. This is a good, important structural feature of the economy. The median value of the economic freedom index for states initially declined from 0.38 in 2005 to 0.36 in 2009, but then rose to 0.43 in 2011.

Gujarat has shown by far the best performance in economic freedom. Its score has risen from 0.46 in *EFSI 2005* to 0.65 in *EFSI 2013*, by far the biggest increased among states (see Table 1.2). It has improved its ranking among

Table 1.2

Overall Economic Freedom Ratings for Indian States

States	2005		2009		2011		2013	
	Overall	*Rank*	*Overall*	*Rank*	*Overall*	*Rank*	*Overall*	*Rank*
Gujarat	0.46	5	0.57	2	0.64	1	0.65	1
Tamil Nadu	0.57	1	0.59	1	0.57	2	0.54	2
Andhra Pradesh	0.40	7	0.51	3	0.51	6	0.50	3
Haryana	0.47	4	0.47	4	0.55	4	0.49	4
Himachal Pradesh	0.48	3	0.43	5	0.52	5	0.47	5
Madhya Pradesh	0.49	2	0.42	6	0.56	3	0.47	6
Rajasthan	0.37	12	0.4	7	0.43	8	0.46	7
Chhattisgarh	0.33	16	0.33	15	0.41	11	0.44	8
Karnataka	0.36	13	0.34	13	0.42	9	0.43	9
Kerala	0.38	10	0.36	10	0.42	10	0.42	10
Maharashtra	0.40	9	0.36	10	0.39	13	0.42	11
Jammu & Kashmir	0.34	15	0.38	8	0.46	7	0.41	12
Punjab	0.41	6	0.35	12	0.39	12	0.40	13
Uttarakhand	0.33	17	0.26	19	0.38	14	0.39	14
Odisha	0.37	11	0.31	17	0.34	17	0.36	15
Uttar Pradesh	0.35	14	0.34	13	0.35	16	0.36	16
West Bengal	0.31	18	0.33	15	0.32	18	0.35	17
Jharkhand	0.40	8	0.38	8	0.31	19	0.33	18
Assam	0.30	19	0.29	18	0.36	15	0.32	19
Bihar	0.25	20	0.23	20	0.29	20	0.31	20

Table 1.3

Areas under Central and State Control in India

Under State Control	*Under Central Control*	*Under Joint Control*
Law, order, justice, local governance	Defence, foreign affairs	Inter-state interactions
Public health, agriculture	Quality standards for public services	Labour issues
Land and water	Rail, ports, airports, posts, national highways	Education
Sales tax, many minor taxes	Income tax, customs and excise taxes	Environment
Local infrastructure	Money, banking, public debt	Power, roads
Some aspects of commerce and industry	Natural resources	Shipping, inland waterways

states from fifth position in 2005 to top position today, and its score of 0.64 is well clear of the others—Tamil Nadu comes second some distance behind with 0.57, which is no higher than its score back in 2005. Bihar remains at the bottom of league, but its score has improved significantly from 0.25 to 0.31, and this improvement in percentage terms is heartening. Chapter 2 examines Bihar's economic performance in greater detail. Jharkhand remains the one state where economic freedom has fallen substantially, from 0.40 in 2005 to 0.33 in 2011.

Our economic freedom index draws on EFW's methodology, and this means that our ratings from Indian states are to some extent comparable to country ratings of EFW. However, given Indian conditions and the manner in which responsibilities are shared between New Delhi and the states (see Table 1.3), only three of the five parameters used by EFW can be adapted for our purposes. In these three areas, the states have enough powers to directly impact outcomes, and so can be rated. The three areas are:

1. Size of government: expenditures, taxes and enterprises.
2. Legal structure and security of property rights.
3. Regulation of labour and business.

While the categories have been included in the index on the lines of the EFW reports, the variables from the EFW could not be replicated at the sub-national level in India. So proxies have been taken wherever possible that are more meaningful at the state level. Often data were unavailable, in which case those indicators had to be eliminated from the study. A detailed table that correlates the indicators used in EFW and those included in the study is presented in Appendix III. The methodology adopted for creating the index is discussed in the following section.

This chapter discusses the outline of the methodology initially. Further, it takes up each of the areas under consideration, describes the variables used and the motivation, and finally discusses the results. The last section of this chapter discusses the overall trends and its significance for economic growth in India.

Methodology in Brief

A detailed methodology is presented in the Appendix II. Here we briefly outline the process. Since data need to be comparable across time and geography, be credible and robust, and highly reflective of the conditions in different states, the following criteria have been identified in selection process of relevant variables.

1. The data should be objective: This signifies that the data should not be based on perceptions but on hard facts so that it is not sensitive to perceptions of the masses, but should reflect the existing factual conditions.

2. Data should be available from highly accepted, public and ideally government or semi-government sources. This would ensure that the ensuing discussion and debate should focus on the resultant performance of the states and not on the quality and credibility of the data.

3. The data should be available periodically and should be available from the same source for different states: This would ensure the credibility of the data and the continuity of the ratings.

Each of the variables constructed is normalised to correct for the differences in the size of the states. Hence normalisation is done through dividing by population, area, a ratio or using it as a percentage of some aggregate so that it is neutral to the size of the state. Moreover, each data source needs to be available for a large enough number of states so that missing data points are minimised.

In line with the previous ratings for the Indian states, the range equalisation method with equal weights has been chosen as the appropriate method. This is a multi-stage process. The first stage of range equalisation is conducted on each variable across all states—this requires subtraction of the minimum value across states from the observation value for each state and dividing the resultant with the difference between the maximum and minimum values. Range equalisation ensures that all variables lie between 0 and 1. In the next stage, each of the new 'range equalised' variables is aggregated with others using equal weights to create an index for each of the areas under consideration. Next, the indices of each of the three areas are aggregated to obtain a composite index using equal weights. Thus, four indices are generated and the states are ranked based on each of these indices.

Area 1: Size of Government: Expenditures, Taxes and Enterprises

Interference of the government in the functioning of the economy or a large role of the government as a producer and provider of services and goods or as a redistributor of resources reduces the level of economic freedom. Government revenue expenditure, administrative GDP and a relatively large employment in the public sector are therefore indicators of size of the government. Taxes on income, commodities and services, property and capital transactions, and other duties are indicative of the extensive role played by the government in the Indian economy.

1) *Inverse of Government Revenue Expenditure as a Share of Gross State Domestic Product (GSDP)*

Higher revenue expenditure by the government is indicative of a larger government size and is thus an indicator of lower economic freedom. Therefore, the inverse of this ratio has been considered.

2) *Inverse of Administrative GSDP as a Ratio of Total GSDP*

Administrative GDP is the contribution of government services to the national product. The lower this ratio, the better is the level of economic freedom as the government's role is lower; therefore, the inverse of this ratio is used.

3) *Inverse of Share of the Government in Organised Employment*

This is the ratio of employment with the government and quasi-government institutions to total organised sector employment. This ratio is a direct indicator of the size of the government. The inverse of the ratio is considered.

4) *Inverse of State-level Taxes on Income as a Ratio of GDP*

This is the ratio of income tax collected by the state to state GDP. Lower the state taxes on income, the higher will be the economic freedom. Therefore, the inverse of this ratio has been incorporated in the analysis.

5) *Inverse of the Ratio of State-level Taxes on Property and Capital Transactions to State GDP*

This is the ratio of taxes on property and capital transactions to state GDP. High transaction costs and taxes tend to restrict the trade activities. Therefore, economic freedom is considered to be inversely related to level of taxation and the inverse of the variable has been taken.

6) *Inverse of State-level Taxes on Commodities and Services to GDP*

This is the ratio of taxes collected on commodities and services i.e., sales tax, service tax, excise, etc., to state GDP. Lower taxes on commodities would result in a higher freedom index score. Hence, the inverse of this ratio has been used.

7) *Inverse of Stamp Duty Rate*

Stamp duty is defined as tax collected by the state by requiring a stamp to be purchased and attached on the commodity. Higher duties impose higher constraints on trade and economic activities and curb the economic freedom of agents. The inverse of this variable is taken to ensure that a higher level of economic freedom is reflected by a higher ratio.

Based on these parameters, the ranking of different states in regard to 'size of government' is shown in Table 1.4.

Haryana ranks first in relation to size of government. It has also been one of the most rapidly growing states of India, and has attracted large investments in the services sector and in manufacturing. Proximity to

Table 1.4

Size of Government: State Scores and Rankings

States	*2005*		*2009*		*2011*		*2013*	
	Area 1	*Rank*	*Area 1*	*Rank*	*Area 1*	*Rank*	*Area 1*	*Rank*
Haryana	0.50	7	0.63	3	0.75	1	0.74	1
Gujarat	0.56	2	0.69	1	0.74	2	0.69	2
Maharashtra	0.52	4	0.53	6	0.68	3	0.68	3
Himachal Pradesh	0.58	1	0.48	10	0.56	10	0.62	4
West Bengal	0.52	4	0.58	4	0.61	7	0.62	5
Andhra Pradesh	0.39	12	0.49	8	0.58	8	0.59	6
Jharkhand	0.56	3	0.67	2	0.50	14	0.59	7
Assam	0.41	11	0.51	7	0.63	4	0.58	8
Punjab	0.49	8	0.54	5	0.61	6	0.58	9
Tamil Nadu	0.46	9	0.47	11	0.57	9	0.57	10
Jammu & Kashmir	0.31	20	0.43	14	0.63	5	0.54	11
Rajasthan	0.34	18	0.44	12	0.50	15	0.54	12
Kerala	0.51	6	0.49	8	0.54	12	0.53	13
Bihar	0.38	16	0.44	12	0.54	11	0.52	14
Odisha	0.32	19	0.38	15	0.44	18	0.50	15
Karnataka	0.38	15	0.36	16	0.48	16	0.49	16
Uttarakhand	0.39	13	0.25	20	0.45	17	0.48	17
Chhattisgarh	0.37	17	0.32	19	0.53	13	0.47	18
Uttar Pradesh	0.45	10	0.33	18	0.40	20	0.38	19
Madhya Pradesh	0.39	14	0.35	17	0.42	19	0.38	20

Delhi, one of India's fastest growing economic centres, would have helped, and Haryana has been able to leverage this without much increase in the size of its government. However, after a big improvement between 2005 and 2011, there has been a marginal decline.

Gujarat is a well-known success story through much of the 2000s. Moreover, it has had major successes in agriculture, social welfare programmes and water resource management. As in Haryana, all of this is being achieved without an inordinate increase in the size of the government. Maharashtra is another state that is among the better performers in this area; the size of the government has not increased as much as economic growth in recent years.

While the top three states have retained their position since 2011, Himachal Pradesh has emerged as one of the top performers in 2013. It has moved up from 10th rank in 2011 to 4th rank in 2013. Assam's index values and rankings which showed significant improvement in 2011, moving up to 4th rank, have again slipped back to 8th rank in 2013. Primarily the high growth of revenue expenditure in comparison to the slow growth of GSDP of the state led to the significant decline in index values.

Jammu & Kashmir and Chhattisgarh had a major set-back this year. Other states which followed suit are Madhya Pradesh, Bihar, Punjab, Uttar Pradesh and Kerala. In all of these states, growth in GDP has not been commensurate with the increase in the size of the government.

Overall there has been some improvement in this category in the period 2005-2011 with the average index values increasing from 0.44 in 2005 to 0.47 in 2009 and to 0.56 in 2011. However, in 2013 there has been a marginal decline in the index value to 0.55. Significant increases in taxes on property and capital transaction compared to slow growth of GDP in most of the states has led to this decline.

Area 2: Legal Structure and Security of Property Rights

The efficiency of the government in protecting human life and property is measured by this category. The quality of the justice mechanism is measured by the availability of judges, by the completion rate of cases by courts and investigations by the police. The level of safety in the region is measured by the recovery rate of stolen property, and by the rate of violent and economic crimes.

8) Ratio of Total Value of Property Recovered to Total Value of Property Stolen

One of the key ingredients of economic freedom is protection of property. This is the ratio of total value of property recovered to the total value of property stolen. A higher value of this variable denotes efficiency of law enforcing agencies in protecting property rights and would therefore signify greater economic freedom.

9) *Inverse of Violent Crimes as a Share of Total Crimes*

This is the ratio of violent crimes, including murder, attempt to murder, etc., to total crimes under the Indian Penal Code (IPC). The inverse of this ratio is considered, relating higher economic freedom to lower incidence of violent crimes.

10) *Inverse of Cases under Economic Offences as a Share of Total Cases Registered*

This is the ratio of economic offences (criminal breach of trust and cheating) to total crimes reported under the IPC. The inverse of this ratio is considered, as lower incidence of economic offences is indicative of better protection of property rights and therefore higher economic freedom.

11) *Inverse of Vacant Posts of Judges in the Judiciary as a Ratio of Total Sanctioned Posts of Judges*

This is the ratio of total vacant posts of judges in district/subordinate courts to total posts sanctioned. A high value of the ratio indicates that adequate infrastructure for getting justice is not in place. Therefore, the inverse of this ratio is considered.

12) *Percentage of Cases where Investigations were Completed by the Police*

This is the ratio of total cases where investigations were completed by the police to total cases registered for investigation by them. A higher value of this ratio indicates higher economic freedom as it indicates lower pendency of investigations.

13) *Percentage of Cases where Trials were Completed by Courts*

This is the ratio of total trials completed by the courts to total cases undergoing trial by courts. A higher value indicates higher economic freedom as it indicates lower pendency of cases.

Based on these parameters, the scores and rankings of the states in Area 2 are shown in Table 1.5.

Madhya Pradesh is one of the best governed states in this respect, and this is reflected in an index value that is well ahead of all others (see Table 1.5). Better police investigations as well as a lower share of economic offences to total incidences of crime keep the state ahead of others. However, compared to the previous year, there has been a low rate of recovery of

Table 1.5

Legal Structure and Security: State Ratings and Rankings

States	*2005*		*2009*		*2011*		*2013*	
	Area 2	*Rank*	*Area 2*	*Rank*	*Area 2*	*Rank*	*Area 2*	*Rank*
Madhya Pradesh	0.63	2	0.62	2	0.83	1	0.62	1
Tamil Nadu	0.80	1	0.90	1	0.64	2	0.55	2
Rajasthan	0.49	5	0.54	4	0.53	3	0.55	3
Andhra Pradesh	0.48	7	0.56	3	0.49	5	0.50	4
Chhattisgarh	0.48	6	0.52	6	0.43	7	0.47	5
Punjab	0.42	9	0.34	10	0.38	11	0.43	6
Jammu & Kashmir	0.35	14	0.32	13	0.29	14	0.39	7
Haryana	0.58	3	0.45	7	0.42	8	0.39	8
Gujarat	0.35	12	0.54	4	0.52	4	0.39	9
Uttar Pradesh	0.41	10	0.39	9	0.38	10	0.37	10
Karnataka	0.45	8	0.34	10	0.36	12	0.35	11
Himachal Pradesh	0.51	4	0.42	8	0.41	9	0.33	12
Kerala	0.35	13	0.34	10	0.45	6	0.31	13
Odisha	0.37	11	0.23	16	0.26	15	0.26	14
Uttarakhand	0.28	15	0.29	14	0.31	13	0.24	15
Jharkhand	0.19	18	0.24	15	0.17	16	0.20	16
Maharashtra	0.26	16	0.19	17	0.15	19	0.16	17
West Bengal	0.20	17	0.15	19	0.16	18	0.14	18
Assam	0.14	19	0.17	18	0.17	17	0.13	19
Bihar	0.12	20	0.11	20	0.08	20	0.12	20

the value of property stolen. This has resulted in a significant decline of its index value. Tamil Nadu remains in 2nd position. It used to be the top state in 2005 and 2009, when its index scores were as high as 0.80 and 0.90 respectively. Its score is a now down to 0.55. This is a widespread problem: more than half the states have shown a declining trend, a sign of growing misgovernance and deteriorating economic freedom.

Rajasthan, Gujarat, Andhra Pradesh, have shown some improvement in their ratings compared with 2005. However, this improvement has not been steady, and there has been significant volatility. Gujarat, which on many parameters is a well-governed state, has shown a steep fall in its score to just 0.39.

Looking at changes since 2011, Bihar, Jammu & Kashmir and Punjab have shown the most improvement. However, despite substantial improvement in police investigations in Bihar, the state continues to be at the bottom of the league, a sad commentary on its low base. Punjab's index scores have been rising over time, and these have been reflected in a sharp improvement in its ranking from 11th position in 2011 to 6th position today. This improvement is mainly on account of a higher rate of recovery of stolen property, a lower ratio of violent crimes to total crime and higher rate of completion of court cases.

On the other hand, Madhya Pradesh, Kerala and Uttarakhand have suffered a significant decline in their index values since 2011. Poor police investigations and low rates of recovery of stolen property are factors leading to this decline.

Ten of the 20 states have fared worse in this 2013 report than in 2011, and overall too there is a marginal decline. This is especially worrisome for some states like West Bengal and Assam, which were among the poorest performers in 2011 too.

The ratings tell a sombre story: the states have been unable to improve security of life and property in the manner required. This puts a serious question mark against the sustainability of high economic growth in such states.

Area 3: Regulation of Labour and Business

An entrepreneur needs to take many decisions that may be opposed by his workers and managers. Decisions such as the right-sizing of employees are essential for efficient use of scarce resources. Constraints on worker exit can seriously hamper an entrepreneur's freedom. Labour laws for many decades have favoured excessive security for workers (in companies with more than 100 employees, no worker can be sacked save with permission from the State Labour Ministry). The number of strikes and industrial disputes is a parameter that reflects economic freedom in terms of the control that an entrepreneur has over his own business. Other areas where an entrepreneur may lack control over his own business relate to inadequate infrastructure. High transactions costs are well-known deterrents to efficient trade and economic activity, and can also contribute to black market transactions. The higher the cost of business in the form of licences and clearances, the more they constrain economic freedom. And, of course, corruption is a widespread problem that translates into higher transactions costs and lower economic freedom.

The following are the parameters we measure to determine economic freedom in relation to the regulation of labour and business.

14) Ratio of Average Wage of Unskilled Workers (Males) to Minimum Wages

This is the ratio of the yearly average of daily wages for crop harvesting to minimum agricultural wages in a state. A value greater than one means that effective wages are higher than the minimum wage, implying undistorted labour markets and hence greater economic freedom both for the entrepreneur and worker.

15) Ratio of Average Wage of Unskilled Workers (Females) to Minimum Wages

Since discrimination against females is widespread, and seriously affects economic freedom, we measure this ratio separately for females and males.

16) Inverse of Man-days Lost in Strikes and Lockouts/ Total Number of Industrial Workers

This is the ratio of man-days lost due to disputes (strikes and lockouts) to the total number of workers. A high ratio indicates a breakdown of arbitration and other consensus-promoting mechanisms. The fewer the man-days lost, the better is economic freedom. Hence we measure the inverse of this ratio.

17) Implementation Rate of Industrial Entrepreneurs Memorandum (IEM)

An IEM denotes an intention to invest in an industry. However, when there are serious bureaucratic or other delays, the rate of implementation is low. We measure the ratio of sums actually invested to the total proposed through IEMs. A high ratio implies fewer bureaucratic hurdles and hence more economic freedom. However, in many cases investors are known to simply sign IEMs to keep Chief Ministers in good humour, without any serious investment intent. To that extent, the implementation rate of IEMs may not reflect speed of clearance.

18) Inverse of Minimum Licence Fee for Traders

Traders are required to pay licence fees for market activities. The higher the license fees, the more restrictive are trading conditions and entry into business. The inverse of this ratio has been adopted in this report, since a higher inverse of the ratio denotes more economic freedom.

19) Inverse of Power Shortage as a Percentage of Total Demand

Power shortages are caused either by low investment by the government (which is by far the largest generator of electricity) or by low levels of private sector generation. Power shortages slow down industrial production, and in fact all business activity. This constrains the ability of entrepreneurs to control their businesses. Again, the inverse of the ratio is taken.

20) Inverse of Pendency Rate of Cases Registered under Corruption and Related Acts

This is the ratio of cases pending investigation from the previous year of cases registered under the Prevention of Corruption Act and other related acts as a share of total cases registered under the same acts. Economic freedom is higher when justice is prompt. Hence, the inverse of the pendency rate is used.

Based on these parameters, the rankings of different states in relation to Area 3 are shown in Table 1.6.

Gujarat has consistently been the best state in this area. It has also recorded the maximum improvement in index score since 2011, and its score of 0.87 is far ahead of Tamil Nadu (0.51) which occupies 2nd position. A host of factors have contributed to Gujarat's continuing improvement. A sharp decline in man-days lost due to strikes and lock-outs, higher market

Table 1.6

Regulation of Labour and Business: State Ratings and Rankings

States	2005		2009		2011		2013	
	Area 3	Rank	Area 3	Rank	Area 3	Rank	Area 3	Rank
Gujarat	0.47	1	0.49	1	0.67	1	0.87	1
Tamil Nadu	0.46	2	0.41	3	0.51	3	0.51	2
Himachal Pradesh	0.36	7	0.38	5	0.63	2	0.46	3
Uttarakhand	0.31	12	0.24	14	0.40	9	0.46	4
Karnataka	0.24	17	0.32	8	0.43	8	0.44	5
Maharashtra	0.41	6	0.35	6	0.36	10	0.43	6
Kerala	0.28	15	0.25	12	0.27	15	0.42	7
Andhra Pradesh	0.33	10	0.48	2	0.45	6	0.40	8
Madhya Pradesh	0.46	3	0.27	11	0.44	7	0.40	9
Chhattisgarh	0.14	20	0.14	20	0.28	14	0.39	10
Haryana	0.32	11	0.34	7	0.47	5	0.34	11
Odisha	0.43	5	0.31	9	0.33	11	0.33	12
Uttar Pradesh	0.18	19	0.3	10	0.28	13	0.32	13
Jammu & Kashmir	0.35	8	0.39	4	0.48	4	0.30	14
Bihar	0.26	16	0.15	19	0.24	17	0.30	15
Rajasthan	0.28	14	0.22	16	0.25	16	0.29	16
West Bengal	0.20	18	0.25	12	0.24	19	0.29	17
Assam	0.34	9	0.19	17	0.28	12	0.26	18
Jharkhand	0.45	4	0.24	14	0.24	18	0.20	19
Punjab	0.30	13	0.18	18	0.22	20	0.19	20

wage rates compared with minimum wage rates, and a decline in pendency of cases are some major factors.

Kerala is another state that has sharply improved its index value, from 0.27 to 0.42 in two years. A significant increase in the market wage rate is a major reason. This state in past decades used to push minimum wages far ahead of market realities. But growing prosperity in the last decade has sent market wages well above the minimum wage.

On the other hand, Himachal Pradesh and Jammu & Kashmir have suffered a significant decline in their index values in 2013 compared with 2011. Power shortages are contributory factors. However, new hydroelectric projects in these states should alleviate the problem.

Uttar Pradesh was second-worst in 2005 (at 19th position) and has now improved to 13th position. It has shown a much improved performance in registration of cases under the Prevention of Corruption Act.

Jharkhand occupied a high 4th position back in 2005, but has crashed now to 19th position. It has performed badly on several parameters, notably wage rates, industrial strife, and cases registered under the Prevention of Corruption Act.

Overall, the average index value for all 20 states declined from 0.33 in 2005 to 0.30 in 2009, but has now improved to 0.38 in 2013. Himachal Pradesh, Andhra Pradesh, Madhya Pradesh, Haryana, Jammu & Kashmir, Assam, Jharkhand and Punjab experienced a decline in their index after 2011, while others showed an improvement.

Overall Ratings

The overall ratings for states are simple equally weighted averages of the ratings in the three areas. The top three states are Gujarat, Tamil Nadu and Andhra Pradesh. These are followed by Haryana, Himachal Pradesh and Madhya Pradesh (see Table 1.7). Gujarat has not only stayed on top but significantly improved its overall rating from 0.46 in 2005 to 0.65 in 2013, driven mainly by better legal and regulatory performance. Tamil Nadu is well behind in 2nd place with a score of 0.54. It used to be in top position in 2005 (with a score of 0.57) as well as in 2009 (0.59), but has since deteriorated, and fallen behind Gujarat. Andhra Pradesh has moved up from 6th rank in 2011 to 3rd rank in 2013, not because of any improvement in its index value but because some other states (Himachal Pradesh, Haryana and Madhya Pradesh) suffered a significant fall.

As many as seven states have suffered a fall in their economic freedom ratings in 2013 compared with 2011. The worst performers in 2013 are Bihar, Jharkhand, Assam and West Bengal. While Bihar, Jharkhand and West Bengal had shown some positive growth in their index ratings since 2011,

Table 1.7

Overall Economic Freedom Ratings

States	2005		2009		2011		2013	
	Overall	*Rank*	*Overall*	*Rank*	*Overall*	*Rank*	*Overall*	*Rank*
Gujarat	0.46	5	0.57	2	0.64	1	0.65	1
Tamil Nadu	0.57	1	0.59	1	0.57	2	0.54	2
Andhra Pradesh	0.40	7	0.51	3	0.51	6	0.50	3
Haryana	0.47	4	0.47	4	0.55	4	0.49	4
Himachal Pradesh	0.48	3	0.43	5	0.52	5	0.47	5
Madhya Pradesh	0.49	2	0.42	6	0.56	3	0.47	6
Rajasthan	0.37	12	0.4	7	0.43	8	0.46	7
Chhattisgarh	0.33	16	0.33	15	0.41	11	0.44	8
Karnataka	0.36	13	0.34	13	0.42	9	0.43	9
Kerala	0.38	10	0.36	10	0.42	10	0.42	10
Maharashtra	0.40	9	0.36	10	0.39	13	0.42	11
Jammu & Kashmir	0.34	15	0.38	8	0.46	7	0.41	12
Punjab	0.41	6	0.35	12	0.39	12	0.40	13
Uttarakhand	0.33	17	0.26	19	0.38	14	0.39	14
Odisha	0.37	11	0.31	17	0.34	17	0.36	15
Uttar Pradesh	0.35	14	0.34	13	0.35	16	0.36	16
West Bengal	0.31	18	0.33	15	0.32	18	0.35	17
Jharkhand	0.40	8	0.38	8	0.31	19	0.33	18
Assam	0.30	19	0.29	18	0.36	15	0.32	19
Bihar	0.25	20	0.23	20	0.29	20	0.31	20

Assam has gone further down. Other states with declining index values in this period are Tamil Nadu, Himachal Pradesh, Haryana, Madhya Pradesh and Jammu & Kashmir. Bihar has not been able to break out of the bottom position it has always held, but its score has improved significantly, from 0.25 in 2005 to 0.31 in 2013.

Compared with 2005, Gujarat has shown the steepest growth. On the other hand, Jharkhand, Madhya Pradesh, Tamil Nadu, Punjab and Odisha have experienced declines in index value.

Overall, the median value for economic freedom of the states of India decreased from 0.38 in 2005 to 0.36 in 2009 but improved in 2013 to 0.43. The overall increase is due mainly to improvements in Area 1 (Size of government) and Area 3 (Regulation of labour and business).

As India opens its national markets to international investment and commodity flows, it cannot afford to constrain its own entrepreneurs.

Table 1.8

Economic Growth and Economic Freedom in Indian States

States	GSDP at 2004-05 Price (₹ '000 crore) in 2004-05	GSDP at 2004-05 Price (₹ '000 crore) in 2011-12	Annual % Growth	Index Values of 2005	Rank in 2005	Index Values in 2013	Rank in 2013	Change in EF Index (2005 to 2013)	Change in Rank (2005 to 2011)	Position in 2005
States with Large Decline	**392**	**731**	**9.3%**							
Jharkhand	60	96	7.0%	0.40	8	0.33	18	(0.07)	10	High
Tamil Nadu	219	433	10.2%	0.57	1	0.54	2	(0.03)	1	High
Madhya Pradesh	113	201	8.6%	0.49	2	0.47	6	(0.02)	4	High
States with Moderate Decline	**199**	**329**	**7.5%**					-		
Punjab	97	156	7.1%	0.41	6	0.40	13	(0.01)	7	High
Himachal Pradesh	24	42	8.3%	0.48	3	0.47	5	(0.01)	2	High
Orissa	78	131	7.7%	0.37	11	0.36	15	(0.01)	4	Low
States with Moderate Rise	**826**	**1,468**	**8.6%**					-		
Uttar Pradesh	261	422	7.1%	0.35	14	0.36	16	0.01	2	Low
Haryana	96	178	9.3%	0.47	4	0.49	4	0.02	-	High
Maharashtra	415	787	9.6%	0.40	9	0.42	11	0.02	2	High
Assam	53	80	6.0%	0.30	19	0.32	19	0.02	-	Low
States with Large Rise	**1,228**	**2,185**	**8.6%**					-		
West Bengal	209	329	6.7%	0.31	18	0.35	17	0.04	(1)	Low
Kerala	119	210	8.4%	0.38	10	0.42	10	0.04	-	Low
Bihar	78	144	9.2%	0.25	20	0.31	20	0.06	-	Low
Uttaranchal	25	59	13.1%	0.33	17	0.39	14	0.06	(3)	Low
Karnataka	167	286	8.0%	0.36	13	0.43	9	0.07	(4)	Low
Jammu & Kashmir	27	41	5.8%	0.34	15	0.41	12	0.07	(3)	Low
Rajasthan	128	228	8.6%	0.37	12	0.46	7	0.09	(5)	Low
Andhra Pradesh	225	405	8.8%	0.40	7	0.50	3	0.10	(4)	High
Chhattisgarh	48	85	8.5%	0.33	16	0.44	8	0.11	(8)	Low
Gujarat	203	400	10.1%	0.46	5	0.65	1	0.19	(4)	High

Economic freedom needs to be improved at the national, state and local levels.

Economic Freedom and Fast Growth

The biggest improvements in overall economic freedom scores during the period under consideration (see Table 1.8) have been registered by Gujarat (0.19 points), Chhattisgarh (0.11 points) and Andhra Pradesh (0.10 points). All three have also registered high levels of growth in state GDP, averaging

10.1 per cent in Gujarat, 8.5 per cent in Chhattisgarh and 8.8 per cent in Andhra Pradesh during the period 2004-05 and 2011-12.

The fastest growth has been recorded by the small hill state of Uttarakhand (annual rate of 13.1 per cent), but this cannot be ascribed to the moderate rise in its economic freedom score by 0.06 points. Rather, its breakneck growth occurred largely because the central government gave an excise duty holiday for all manufacturing units set up in the state till 2010, supposedly to compensate it for its hilly terrain. This was a classic case of bad policy. Industries rushed into the state to take advantage of the tax breaks, but almost all set up shop in the thin strip of plains in the south of the state, and virtually none went to the hilly regions. With the end of the tax break, growth in the state is going to slow rapidly, and it will have to look to better policies for powering its future growth. Bihar has been among the fastest growing states, averaging 9.2 per cent growth between 2004-05 and 2011-12. Its freedom score has improved only moderately by 0.06 points. But in percentage terms, this is a significant improvement of almost 25 per cent from a very low base. Besides, our indicators do not capture some of the improvements in economic freedom in Bihar due to the reduction of gangsterism and taming of Maoism, and the consequent improvement in the investment climate (see Chapter 2 on Bihar's performance).

The worst performance in economic freedom comes from Jharkhand, with a decline in score of 0.07 points. It has also been the fourth slowest growing state, averaging just 7.0 per cent. It used to be part of the composite Bihar state till 2000, and when that was split, Jharkhand found itself with all the coal, iron ore, major industrial cities and the bulk of tax revenue of the old composite state. Yet because of better policies and more economic freedom, Bihar has grown fast while Jharkhand (with gross mis-governance and falling economic freedom) has grown less rapidly.

The slowest growing state has been Jammu & Kashmir (5.8 per cent per year). Its economic freedom score has improved by 0.07 points, but the state continues to be dogged by terrorism. A similar tale can be told of Assam, the state with the second slowest growth (6.0 per cent). Its economic freedom score has risen a smidgeon, by 0.02 points. But it suffers from multiple insurgencies (from groups like the United Liberation Front of Assam and Bodoland People's Party) and high corruption, which hamper progress. Other states such as Punjab, Tamil Nadu and Odisha have had a moderate fall in their ratings (0 to 0.02 points). On the other hand, Rajasthan Kerala, Karnataka, West Bengal, Haryana, Maharashtra, Himachal Pradesh and Uttar Pradesh have seen moderate improvements (ranging from 0.01 to 0.09 points).

The states that have improved the most have improved in a wide range of indicators. This drives home the points that improvements in economic freedom require wide-ranging reforms, not just excellent performance in one or two areas.

2

Bihar

How the Poorest, Worst-Governed State Attained Double-Digit Growth and Became a Role Model

Swaminathan S. Anklesaria Aiyar

Introduction

Bihar has long been India's poorest, most backward state, riddled with misgovernance, caste wars, gangsterism, Maoism and hopelessness. Its institutional weaknesses have made it a figure of fun. There was an old joke that when British India was being partitioned in 1947 (to create the two independent states of India and Pakistan), Indian Prime Minister Nehru told his Pakistani counterpart that he could have the disputed state of Kashmir provided he took Bihar and Uttar Pradesh too. These two states, with a combined population today of over 300 million, were seen as a terrible drag on the rest of India, having some of the lowest growth rates and social indicators among Indian states.

Yet Bihar has undergone a veritable revolution since a new dynamic Chief Minister, Nitish Kumar, came to power in 2005 (and was re-elected in 2010 with a landslide majority). If we look at data available for the last six years from 2006-07 to 2011-12, Bihar averaged GDP growth rate of a whopping 10.87 per cent. This was the highest among major states (some mini-states fared even better), and well above the national average of 8.29 per cent.[1] So Bihar, which was historically a drag on the rest of India, has started pulling up the rest of India. This merits international attention because Bihar has a population of 100 million, more than that of all except a handful of countries. Unlike some other developmental successes, Bihar's is not a boutique success: it is success on a grand scale. However, despite this sharp improvement, consumption (measured by per capita monthly rural spending) remains close to the lowest among all states, an indicator of how far behind Bihar has long been, and continues to be (Table 2.1).

Table 2.1

Consumption and Poverty in Major Indian States

	Rural Monthly Per Capita Consumption (₹)	*Poverty Headcount Ratio (%)*
Andhra Pradesh	1,563	9.20
Assam	1,057	31.98
Bihar	970	33.74
Chhattisgarh	904	39.93
Gujarat	1,430	16.63
Haryana	1,801	11.16
Jammu & Kashmir	1,602	10.35
Jharkhand	919	36.96
Karnataka	1,395	20.91
Madhya Pradesh	1,024	31.65
Maharashtra	1,446	17.35
Odisha	905	32.59
Punjab	2,137	8.26
Rajasthan	1,446	14.71
Tamil Nadu	1,570	11.28
Uttar Pradesh	1,072	29.43
West Bengal	1,179	19.98

Source: Press Note on Poverty Estimates 2011-12, Planning Commission.

Fast growth has driven down the headcount poverty ratio in Bihar, which used to be India's poorest state. The ratio was as high as 56 per cent in 2004-05 (which was a serious drought year), and has crashed to just 33.74 per cent in 2011-12. This is a very dramatic decline. So, although its consumption levels remain among the lowest, Bihar has ceased to be India's poorest state—five other states now have a higher poverty headcount ratio (although three of these are tiny mini-states and so not strictly comparable). The all-India poverty ratio also declined sharply in the same period from 37 per cent to 22 per cent, but this decline was not as fast as in Bihar. The all-India performance as well as Bihar's performance showed that, contrary to much leftist theorising, faster growth is indeed a major force in reducing poverty.

Many of the state's social indicators have improved dramatically too. This helps falsify the supposed trade-off between growth and equity. The plain fact is that growth is vital for improving not only incomes but government revenues required for providing public goods (essential infrastructure and social services). Of course, fast growth also requires good governance, to ensure that the new revenues are utilised well. In the decade 2001-2011, Bihar's literacy rate improved 16.8 percentage points and female literacy by a whopping 20 per cent. The state historically had a very high infant mortality rate, but in 2011, Bihar's caught up with the national average at 44 infant deaths per thousand births. Polio, a scourge of the ages, was finally eradicated in Bihar and Uttar Pradesh in 2011 (it had been eradicated in other states much earlier).[2]

Bihar continues to have the least family planning and hence the highest population growth rate (2.1 per cent per year) among major states. But with labour scarcity growing and wages rising fast in India, what used to be condemned as a 'population explosion' is now being hailed as a 'demographic dividend.' Low wages and fast population growth, which historically kept Bihar poor, now promise to give the state a competitive edge and drive fast growth for decades to come.

Development economics is full of fancy theories on how to make developing countries grow fast. In the bad old days of Bihar, many of these theories could be used to explain the state's dismal performance. But its new dynamism after 2005 was based on two main pillars—a crackdown on gangsters and massive road building. One consequence was that the total number of registered vehicles in the state quadrupled from just 80,000 in 2005-06 to 3,19,000 by 2019-10.[3] The taming of crime hugely improved the investment climate, and fast road-building (plus India's broader telecom revolution) suddenly provided economic opportunities in villages that earlier had no infrastructure and hence no opportunities. However, just these two factors, public safety plus roads, would not have produced double-digit GDP growth in Bihar without major all-India reforms since 1991 that helped accelerate growth in all states. The more advanced coastal states were the first to take advantage of new opportunities created by economic liberalisation, but in the last decade, the backward BIMAROU states (acronym for Bihar, Madhya Pradesh, Rajasthan, Odisha and Uttar Pradesh) have began to do the same. Bihar is the best example among BIMAROU states, thanks in no small measure to the dynamism and the improvement in economic freedom Nitish Kumar has brought in as Chief Minister from 2005 onwards.

In the year 2000, Jharkhand was carved out of the original Bihar state. Jharkhand was a thinly-populated, highly-forested tribal belt. In India, tribal areas are often viewed as backward. Yet the partition gave Jharkhand almost all the coal and minerals of the original state, and four major industrial cities and steel mills at Jamshedpur, Ranchi, Bokaro and Sindri. Bihar was left with an overwhelmingly agrarian area, which had a very high population density and tiny land holdings. However, Jharkhand was left with major disadvantages too. It was predominantly a tribal area with dense forest and limited infrastructure, and this offsets to some extent the advantages of mineral deposits and a few industrial cities. But this cannot explain why Jharkhand has even lower per capita expenditure and a higher poverty headcount ratio than Bihar (see Table 2.1). A significant reason for this is massive misgovernance in Jharkhand, and the lack of a dynamic leader like Nitish Kumar. This is reflected in a decline in economic freedom scores in Jharkhand, in contrast to a substantial increase in freedom scores in Bihar.

After partition, Bihar's share of industry in net state domestic product (NSDP) crashed from 22.5 per cent to a calamitously low 4.6 per cent, while that of Jharkhand went up to 37 per cent. The royalties and tax base from minerals and the big industrial cities all went to Jharkhand, leaving Bihar in desperate fiscal straits. Besides, almost all of the original composite state's coal and power stations went to Jharkhand. Bihar has by far the lowest per capita consumption of power (122 kWh) among Indian states, less than one-tenth that of Gujarat, Chhattisgarh or Himachal Pradesh, one reason for its tiny industrial base. New power plants are finally coming up in the state, and hopefully will help correct the current lopsided pattern of development. Be that as it may, Bihar has been an eye-opener in demonstrating how even lopsided development can achieve huge increases in GDP and reductions in poverty in a poor, backward state without electricity.[4]

Annual EFSI reports have long shown a link between economic freedom and fast GDP growth. But Bihar may in some respects look an outlier. Its economic freedom scores continue to be the lowest among states, yet it has been a growth champion. This paradox is examined in greater detail at the end of this chapter. One explanation is that while Bihar's scores remain dismal, they nevertheless show an improvement of almost a quarter since 2005, much faster than the national average. Second, when the state shrinks to the point where it cannot provide physical security or basic infrastructure, it means anarchy and gangster rule. To the extent that gangsters are linked with a corrupt political class, what earlier looked small government in spending terms was actually a huge political footprint that undercuts the rule of law. In such circumstances, the restoration of safety and basic infrastructure produced spectacular growth, even though other indicators of economic freedom did not show dramatic change. A third explanation is that the state enjoyed a huge increase in transfers from the central government in the last decade, thanks in part to the revenue bonanza New Delhi reaped from fast growth catalysed by economic liberalisation.

The Political Economy of Change: From Lalu Yadav to Nitish Kumar

Bihar was historically the seat of many major Indian empires. Its fertile soil and ample rainfall created ideal conditions for agriculture, but also led to explosive population growth and the reduction of farms to ever-tinier sizes. Land ownership under colonial British rule was dominated by *zamindars*, huge landowners belonging to the upper castes. The backward castes and Dalits (once called untouchables) were powerless tenants or quasi-serfs, often on the verge of starvation. Land reform after Indian independence in 1947 aimed to distribute land to lower castes and improve the security of tenants, but was mostly sabotaged by the upper castes (Brahmins, Rajputs and Bhumihars). These upper castes accounted for less than one-third of the population but dominated politics and everything else by virtue of superior wealth and education. The police stations were effectively in the pocket of landowning castes, so rural Bihar remained a feudal zone where the elite could do almost anything to the lower castes (including assault and rape) with almost complete impunity. Unsurprisingly, it became fertile ground for Maoist groups from the 1960s onwards. South Bihar, which has now become the new state of Jharkhand, had thick forests and few roads, and so offered safe sanctuary for Maoists, most of who moved to this region. Fewer Maoists remained in the rump state of Bihar after partition, and their influence has gone down a lot in the last decade, but they are still a force to reckon with.[5]

The clout of the backward Hindu castes rose steadily after Indian independence. In Bihar, from 1970s onwards, these backward castes became the main force of a political new party, the Janata Dal. In 1990, led by Lalu Yadav (belonging to the Yadav or cowherd caste), the party was elected to power. It stayed in power for the next 15 years (it is now called the Rashtriya Janata Dal or RJD). Lalu Yadav formed a strong alliance with the Muslims of the state, showering them with patronage and providing them security from militant Hindus. His Yadav-Muslim combination helped him win election after election. However, backward castes other than the Yadavs found themselves getting politically marginalised and left out of the vast patronage network of Lalu Yadav. These groups broke away under the leadership of Nitish Kumar to form the Janata Dal United (JDU).

Lalu Yadav saw his role as that of providing the lower castes with dignity and power, and putting the upper castes in their place. Yadav's aim was not to end the gross misgovernance and misuse of power by earlier upper-caste governments. Rather, he aimed to misuse the same power to promote his own caste and religious allies, and become as wealthy and as much above the law as upper-caste leaders had been in the past. Crime had long been rampant in this anarchic state, but earlier upper-caste gangs dominated. Most famous was the Ranbir Sena, a motley collection of private militias of upper-caste landowners, which periodically battled low-caste villages organised by the Maoists. Yadav gave protection to his own favoured gangsters, and created his own patronage network that extorted money with impunity.

He did not believe in economic development, which he saw as a ploy long used by upper castes to perpetrate unequal access to power and funds, and to keep other castes down. India's federal structure provided for the sharing of substantial revenues by New Delhi with the states, but Yadav contemptuously returned vast unspent sums, partly because he had no interest in raising matching state funds. The state's road network collapsed. When asked why he did not build more roads, he is reputed to have said "Whose cars will run on such roads, and whose cows will be hit and killed by the cars?" This was the language of caste war, clear and succinct, pitting the upper-caste car owner against the low-caste cattle owner. His language stressed not economic development but caste vengeance, backward-caste control of the levers of power, and a fair share of the spoils of misgovernance once monopolised by the upper castes. This approach had mass appeal for the lower castes, who felt they had now been empowered. Their sense of improved dignity was immediate, and so for some time, it did not matter electorally that this approach kept Bihar poor and lacking in infrastructure.

Governance failure under Yadav was not inevitable because of a combination of high poverty, a low revenue base and step-motherly treatment by New Delhi, as alleged by some analysts. One important study argues that Bihar had "state incapacity by design."[6] Yadav deliberately refused to fill vacant government posts or approve development budgets because the bureaucracy was dominated by the upper castes, and depriving them of budgets and staff strength was seen by Yadav as a way of increasing the political power of his backward-caste politicians, and putting the upper castes in their place. He deliberately humiliated several upper-caste officials in public, to drive home the point. Rather than let the people get services from an empowered bureaucracy, he wanted to create the impression that any government services were favours from the backward-caste government, so that sundry vote banks would be beholden to him alone and not to any abstract entity called the efficient state. Traditionally-oppressed groups, that had obtained very few benefits of development under decades of upper-caste rule, were happy to coalesce behind Yadav and his approach. Matthew and Moore write, "Such was the scale of poverty among this core electoral coalition that Yadav had limited prospects of maintaining its cohesion through the normal processes of promising 'development'... He preferred using networks of personal patronage to distribute material resources to supporters. More important, that 'development' strategy would have involved a high dependence on the government apparatus, that was dominated by people from a number of historically-dominant upper castes."[7]

Yadav's approach proved popular with his favoured vote banks, and was successful electorally for quite some time. He won state elections in 1990, 1995, 2000 and fell only marginally short of power in the election of 2005, which produced a hung state assembly in which no group could form a government. But within a few months, to break the deadlock, a second state election was held, and this time Nitish Kumar and his allies won a clear majority. He and Yadav had been colleagues for decades in the fight against upper-caste domination, so they had much common ground. But Nitish Kumar saw clearly that caste war alone could not make Bihar prosperous, and could not even be an election-winning approach once the novelty of backward-caste rule wore off. He saw that ordinary folk were sick and tired of gangster rule and lack of electricity, roads and jobs. An engineer himself, he saw the need to revive the state's infrastructure. At the same time, as a clever Bihar politician, he saw the need to use caste-based appointments and programmes to woo a wide variety of groups, not backward castes alone. It helped greatly that his main political ally, the Bhartiya Janta Party (BJP), was an upper-caste party, and one also interested in economic development.

Nitish Kumar did not aim for a miracle economy. He merely aimed to woo voters by doing what little he could in very unpromising conditions. During his 2005 election campaign, he declared that his first, second and third priority were all improved governance and physical safety for the common man.[8] He had no idea this would spur record economic growth, and was happily surprised when the state's GDP growth soared to 11 per cent per year. He was somewhat amused to find that while he himself was merely trying to get re-elected, he had unwittingly produced an economic model that was attracting world-wide attention. His successful re-election with a landslide majority in 2010 convinced him that Bihar's voters had evolved well beyond the Yadav model of caste war to promote dignity for the backward castes. Kumar saw the election result as vindication of his focus on improved governance and economic development. He incorporated this in his future vision, for the state as well as his own political future.[9]

A New Path to Miracle Economic Growth

Between 1992 and 2002, under Lalu Yadav, state GDP grew at an average of just 3.8 per cent per year. Then after Nitish Kumar came to power, the state's growth rate more than doubled to 9.34 per cent per year between 2005-06 and 2011-12 (see Table 2.2). However, the first of these years witnessed a major drought that reduced state GDP growth to almost zero. If we leave out this year, we find Bihar's growth rate in the next six years averaged 10.8 per cent per year.[10]

To some extent, this reflected the acceleration of growth across all Indian states. As the country participated in the global economic boom of the times, all-India growth averaged a record 8.46 per cent, up from around

Table 2.2

State GDP Growth (%) at Constant (2004-05) Prices

	Per cent Growth of Gross Domestic Product at Constant (2004-05) Prices							
States/UT	*2005-06*	*2006-07*	*2007-08*	*2008-09*	*2009-10*	*2010-11*	*2011-12*	*Average*
Andhra Pradesh	9.57	11.18	12.02	6.88	4.53	9.66	7.82	8.81
Arunachal Pradesh	2.75	5.25	12.06	8.73	9.86	1.25	10.84	7.25
Assam	3.4	4.65	4.82	5.72	9	7.89	6.47	5.99
Bihar	0.17	15.69	5.72	12.16	7.09	11.29	13.26	9.34
Chhattisgarh	3.23	18.6	8.61	8.39	3.42	9.75	8.14	8.59
Goa	7.54	10.02	5.54	10.02	10.2	10.15	9.39	8.98
Gujarat	14.95	8.39	11	6.78	11.25	10	8.53	10.13
Haryana	9.2	11.22	8.45	8.17	11.72	8.84	7.92	9.36
Himachal Pradesh	8.43	9.09	8.55	7.42	8.09	8.74	7.44	8.25
Jammu & Kashmir	5.78	5.95	6.4	6.46	4.51	5.96	6.22	5.90
Jharkhand	-3.2	2.38	20.52	-1.75	10.14	8.67	8.92	6.53
Karnataka	10.51	9.98	12.6	7.11	1.29	9.66	5.5	8.09
Kerala	10.09	7.9	8.77	5.56	9.17	8.06	9.51	8.44
Madhya Pradesh	5.31	9.23	4.69	12.47	9.88	7.13	11.81	8.65
Maharashtra	13.35	13.53	11.26	2.58	9.17	11.34	8.54	9.97
Manipur	6.35	2	5.96	6.56	6.89	5.07	6.71	5.65
Meghalaya	7.91	7.74	4.51	12.94	6.55	8.72	6.31	7.81
Mizoram	6.97	4.78	10.98	13.34	12.38	7.25	10.09	9.40
Nagaland	10.22	7.8	7.31	6.34	6.9	5.46	5.09	7.02
Odisha	5.68	12.85	10.94	7.75	4.55	7.5	4.92	7.74
Punjab	5.9	10.18	9.05	5.85	6.29	6.53	5.94	7.11
Rajasthan	6.68	11.67	5.14	9.09	6.7	15.28	6.11	8.67
Sikkim	9.78	6.02	7.61	16.39	73.61	8.13	8.17	18.53
Tamil Nadu	13.93	15.21	6.13	4.89	10.36	9.83	7.37	9.68
Tripura	5.82	8.28	7.7	9.44	10.65	8.2	8.67	8.39
Uttar Pradesh	6.51	8.07	7.32	6.99	6.58	7.81	6.86	7.16
Uttarakhand	14.34	13.59	18.12	12.65	18.13	9.94	5.28	13.15
West Bengal	6.29	7.79	7.76	4.9	8.03	9.22	6.58	7.22
Andaman & Nicobar Island	5.18	18.04	10.13	14.32	13.2	8.2	6.14	10.74
Chandigarh	10.69	14.68	7.28	8.1	9.96	8.23	7.11	9.44
Delhi	10.05	12.39	11.19	12.92	10.94	10.92	11.34	11.39
Puducherry	24.92	3.69	8.59	8.66	15.72	10.06	2.4	10.58
All-India GDP (2004-05 base)	9.48	9.57	9.32	6.72	8.59	9.32	6.21	8.46

Source: Central Statistical Organisation, India (website) (as of March 2013).

6 per cent in the preceding decade. But, strikingly, Bihar now grew much faster than the national average. For decades, it had grown more slowly.

Table 2.2 shows that Bihar is not alone among historically backward states in accelerating in the last decade. India has long had a group of backward states with the acronym BIMAROU. These states account for almost half of India's population, but used to be far behind the national average in income, governance, social indicators and growth. Many lacked the financial resources—or governance quality—to provide minimal levels of infrastructure, education and health. When New Delhi liberalised the Indian economy in the 1990s, the advanced states (most of which were coastal) immediately took advantage of the new opportunities of reform and globalisation, but these BIMAROU states failed to accelerate. This led to the theory that economic reform was bad for the backward states and would mean widening disparities that caused social chaos. Yet in the 2000s, the notion that economic reform was bad for the poor, land-locked states was soon disproved. A new bunch of dynamic chief ministers emerged in some of the BIMAROU states, and soon showed that the most backward states were capable of very fast growth in the new milieu. The best-governed BIMAROU states began growing faster than the national average, though the less well-governed ones did not. Bihar did better than any of the big backward states. Note that Uttarakhand, a small hill state hived off from backward Uttar Pradesh in 2000, grew at an average of no less than 13.15 per cent per year (see Table 2.2). In sum, a rising tide in the 2000s lifted all boats in backward states, but some rose much more than others thanks to dynamic new chief ministers like Nitish Kumar.

In the year 2000, three of the BIMAROU states (Bihar, Uttar Pradesh and Madhya Pradesh) were split to create the new states of Jharkhand, Uttarakhand and Chhattisgarh respectively. Bihar was worst hit by the splits. All the mineral-rich areas and industrial towns of the original state went to Jharkhand, leaving the rump Bihar state overwhelmingly agricultural and poor. As noted in the introduction, the share of industry in Bihar's NSDP crashed from 22.5 per cent to a calamitously low 4.6 per cent, while that of Jharkhand went up to 37 per cent. By 2004-05 when Nitish Kumar came to power, Bihar's share of industry had edged up to 6 per cent. But no less than 90 per cent of the population lived in rural areas (against the national average of 70 per cent), and the proportion of the population dependent on agriculture for work was 81 per cent in Bihar, almost double the national average. Deprived of royalties and taxes from minerals and the big industrial cities (all of which went to Jharkhand), Bihar found itself in a desperate financial situation.

Yet after Nitish Kumar assumed office in 2005, growth took off. Agriculture grew strongly, but the economy grew even faster, so agriculture's share fell from 32 per cent in 2004-05 to 18 per cent in 2011-12. This is typically a sign of strong economic evolution. The share of industry remained at around 6 per cent, but that of services shot up from 62 per cent to 77 per cent. This was a very lopsided sort of development, clearly unsustainable in the long run. Far more industrialisation was needed, but was hamstrung by the fact that all the coal and most of the power stations in the composite state went to Jharkhand. Bihar's 100 million people were left with a net power availability of barely 1,500 MW. Even this supply was often not available because of a moribund, bankrupt power transmission network. Attracting private power suppliers was difficult for two reasons. First, no entrepreneur wanted to invest until it became clear that Lalu Yadav was not going to return to power. Second, India has run into a severe coal shortage, with existing power plants rendered idle for want of fuel. Until coal production goes up significantly—and this will probably require the de-nationalisation of coal mines—private investment in power will be limited.[11]

Yet industrial growth has been significant in Bihar even in these terrible conditions (see Table 2.3). Much new industry has been based on expensive power from diesel generating sets, and this is not sustainable beyond a point.

Table 2.3

Bihar: Sectoral Growth (1999-2000 Prices)

Sector	*Annual Growth 2000-2010 (%)*	*Annual Growth 2005-2010 (%)*
Agriculture	-0.20	3.60
Industry	2.00	6.00
Services	8.40	11.90

Source: Mukherji and Mukherji (2013), citing the Central Statistical Organisation.

All investment, building and consumer purchases had been severely curtailed by what was called 'jungle *raj*'—meaning rule of the jungle—in the state under Lalu Yadav. It was said that if you applied to a dealer to buy a car, or to a municipality for building a house, than you would by the evening get a protection money note, threatening kidnapping or worse. Naturally, nobody wanted to buy cars, build houses or start industries. In any case, as the roads deteriorated and virtually disappeared in district after district and the power shortage worsened, there was little sense in attempting industrial investment. Public investment also slumped because Lalu Yadav was not interested in economic development and preferred to focus on caste politics. Unsurprisingly, GDP growth and industrial growth were close to the worst among the states.

The fiscal crunch caused by the partition of the state was used by Yadav as an excuse to keep vacancies remaining unfilled in all government services, not just in education and health but also police, judges and everything else. This further weakened the capacity of a state already crippled by lack of funds. Yet weakening the bureaucracy was, as observed earlier, also a deliberate ploy by Yadav to reduce the power of a bureaucracy dominated by the upper castes. Gangsters linked to Yadav proliferated and prospered, while Maoists proliferated in backward districts.

In 2005, Nitish Kumar did not come to power on a platform of accelerating GDP or industry or electricity output. He stressed above all the need for good governance to check gangsters and Maoism, and bring back some semblance of public safety and functioning public services. In a state long viewed as ungovernable, Kumar showed that a determined chief minister could galvanise the bureaucracy, police and judiciary to start governing again. The level of effort that Kumar demanded required senior officers to work late every night and even on weekends. This created a work ethic unthinkable in the Yadav era.[12]

Kumar called together the top police, judicial and administrative officials, earlier a demoralised and unmotivated lot. He got them to work together on a crash programme for delivering speedy trials and convictions. Earlier, mafia dons proudly exhibited a veritable arsenal of weapons when they travelled with their entourages. Committing murders and kidnappings was seen not as a path to jail but a path to proving your clout and hence becoming a political force. Sociologist Max Weber once said that the state is the only entity that can use force with legal impunity. But when the law itself is moribund, those who can use guns with impunity become, in effect, the state. That's what happened in Bihar.

This was the malaise that Kumar and his team decide to tackle. One strategy was to try criminals not for their worst crimes—this entailed long trials for years, during which witnesses could usually be threatened to keep silent—but for violating the Arms Act, something which could easily be proved and so ensure a conviction within weeks. Later the Bihar Special Courts Act in 2009 legalised fast-track processes for criminal cases. Many strong vested interests sought to sabotage this, but Kumar's determination won the day. Since 2005, around 80,000 gangsters and top criminals have been convicted and jailed. This has produced a sea change in safety. No longer does any gangster boast of his arsenal of weapons. No longer do top gangsters become ministers (as dons like Taslimuddin, Shahbuddin and Papu Yadav did earlier). Even mafia dons with links to the ruling party (like Munna Shukla) have been convicted. Gun-power has ceased to be a route to the legislature, and instead become a route to jail.

Apart from quashing gangsters, Kumar boasts that he has focused on promoting female rights and ensured greater participation for them in all walks of life, including politics. He has given women a 50 per cent quota in local-level *panchayat* elections and a 35 per cent quota in police recruitment. So, some might be impressed by the fact that Bihar, at 14.05 per cent, has by far the highest proportion of female members of the State Legislative Assembly among Indian states (see Table 2.4). But does this really represent elevated female power in this notoriously quasi-feudal state? The picture changes when we also take a look at the proportion of legislators facing criminal charges. Here too Bihar comes out on top, with 35.12 per cent.

What's the connection between the two sets of data? The sad answer is that, as more and more legislators are convicted, they are barred by law from contesting elections. So, they put up their wives as candidates at elections, assuring voters that they (the male dons) will continue to be in charge. The wives duly get elected in areas where the dons have most influence. What looks like high status of women in the legislature is actually a reflection of high criminality among male legislators. The most famous example of such a husband-wife combination is that of Lalu Yadav and his wife Rabri Devi: he made her not just a legislator but chief minister after he himself had to resign after being charged in a scam related to the mass diversion of funds meant for supplying fodder and ruled through her.

Table 2.4

More Legislators Jailed, More of their Wives become Legislators

States/UTs	*% of MLA's with Serious Criminal Charges*	*Percentage of Female MLA's*
Haryana	2.22	10.00
Rajasthan	4.02	14.07
Punjab	4.27	5.98
Assam	7.14	11.11
Kerala	8.57	5.00
Andhra Pradesh	9.45	10.18
Gujarat	9.89	8.80
Chhattisgarh	12.22	12.22
Madhya Pradesh	12.67	9.05
Tamil Nadu	15.81	7.26
Karnataka	17.85	1.30
Uttar Pradesh	18.48	5.82
Maharashtra	19.51	3.83
Odisha	21.09	4.76
West Bengal	25.51	11.56
Jharkhand	32.10	2.47
Bihar	35.12	14.05

Source: Poonam Gupta, National Institute of Public Finance and Policy (NIPFP), comment on "The Quality of Governance: How Have Indian States Performed?", by Sudipto Mundle, Pinaki Chakraborty, Samik Chowdhury, Satadru Sikdar, Presented at NIFPF/Columbia University Seminar, New Delhi, August 7-8, 2012.

Note that this is now a trend in all parties, not just Yadav's party. A feature in the magazine *India Today* says that almost half the 118 elected legislators of Kumar's party face criminal charges. As many as 23 of them face murder charges and 35 attempted murder. In many other cases, Kumar's legislators are wives of politician barred from contesting or in some cases, persuaded by Kumar not to contest. "So, in effect, power in Bihar remains largely vested in Nitish Kumar's loyal dons, directly or indirectly", says the magazine. This criticism is excessive. Kumar does not give these dons free rein to murder and loot, rather, he has reined in their earlier illegal power and given them more modest but legal power. He sees the induction of selected gangsters and their wives as a way of improving governance: this avoids the worst criminality, gives a chance to selected gangsters to reform and is a form of realpolitik, living with the reality that dons still command considerable influence and votes. However, this drives home the lesson that while governance may indeed have improved in Bihar, it has a long way to go.[13]

Kumar introduced an e-governance programme called "Jankari" enabling people to file a right-to-information request online or over the phone. This has activised a right-to-information law that had earlier lain moribund. This quickly introduced a degree of transparency in government decision-making that improved public confidence, and checked some of the most flagrant abuses of power (though by no means all).[14]

Kumar has sought to use development as a way to tame Maoism. Bihar lost most of its jungles (and Maoists) to Jharkhand on being partitioned in 2000. Its remaining Maoists have not been jungle-based guerillas (as in Jharkhand) but activists in settled agricultural areas, where they pose as champions of agricultural labourers against exploitative feudal landowners who ignore all laws. In past decades, Maoists frequently organised strikes at harvest time, when labour is most needed. In retaliation, private armies of the landowning castes—broadly called the Ranbir Sena—often attacked low-caste villages, raping and killing. The Ranbir Sena leaders often evolved into urban dons too. The Maoists in turn attacked upper caste villages, and sometimes over-ran police stations to snatch away modern weapons. The moribund state was a helpless spectator to this caste-cum-class warfare.

Some other states tried to check the Maoist threat through paramilitary forces (as in Andhra Pradesh) or by creating local militia (as in Chhattisgarh). Nitish Kumar chose another path—economic development plus restoration of public order by jailing the worst gangsters. The return of safety, fast expansion of the road network and rapid spread of cell phones all created new economic opportunities, so economic growth galloped upward. Agriculture boomed too and rural wages shot up in response to higher productivity plus a new employment guarantee scheme from New Delhi. The old labour surplus that led to much outmigration from the state was replaced by a labour shortage, not just in richer states but even in Bihar. Wages in many places rose above the legal minimum wage. This eroded the Maoist claim to be the only saviours of the poor: economic development now did more for the poor than Maoist guns. Rural caste battles died down, and the labour shortage actually induced a rapid spread of combine-harvesters.[15]

Rising wages were buttressed by the revival of education. More than 200,000 teachers were hired by Nitish Kumar through an innovative decentralised reform, to revive moribund schools, and this helped literacy soar by almost 17 per cent in 2001-11, the fastest among all states. The number of patients treated per primary health centre rose from an average of just 39 per month to 4,000 per month. Government teachers had long been notorious for high absenteeism, despite high pay. So, Kumar decided to let the new teachers be hired by *panchayats* (local governments) at low, market-related wages. This facilitated a huge expansion of schooling at low cost, but the quality of teachers was also low (many lacked the minimum qualifications). Kumar seeks to upgrade their skills through teacher training. The low-paid local teachers are now agitating to become official state-level teachers, unionised and highly paid. But Kumar plans to hire no more state-level teachers at all, allowing this highly paid cadre to disappear through attrition. The only remaining teachers will be hired by local governments, which in theory are free to discipline or fire them if they fail to teach. This will be a revolutionary reform that shrinks the role of the state government. It may be extended to other government services, like health services.

In the last seven years, the additional 200,000 extra teachers have been supplemented by 100,000 additional classrooms. Upper primary schools have doubled in number from 11,000 in 2004-05 to 25,000 in 2010-11. This greatly helped increase school enrolment. Private schools have also expanded rapidly—the return of economic growth has raised parental aspirations and induced them to shift their children from free government schools to fee-charging private schools (often unlicenced and unrecognised by state authorities) on a large scale. One study suggests that 65 per cent of children in Patna, the state capital, are in private schools. The study looked in Patna for private schools located within a 1-km radius of existing government schools and found a minimum of 9 and maximum of 63 such private schools.[16]

Children in unrecognised schools cannot appear for official school-leaving exams. Yet, the study showed that the majority of parents knew this and did not care. One reason was double enrolment: kids were enrolled in government schools but actually studying in private unaided schools. This was illegal, but enabled them to appear for exams, after greasing some palms. Once again, government failure was partly assuaged by a nominally illegal but socially sanctioned market solution.[17]

For the age-group 6-14 years, the proportion of children out of school declined from 12.8 per cent in 2006 to 3 per cent in 2011. Of the age group 11-14 for girls, the decline was truly dramatic: from 17.6 per cent (second highest among all states) to just 4.3 per cent in 2011 (below the all-India average). The government's elementary school spending doubled, from ₹ 5,600 crore ($933.3 million) in 2006-07 to over ₹ 11,000 crore ($ 1833.3 million) in 2010-11. However, student absenteeism continues to be a serious problem: attendance in government primary and upper primary schools has ranged from 50 per cent to 59 per cent. Inclusive of private schools, which have a better record, attendance is still only 62 per cent. Educational outcomes remain poor: children in class 6 cannot read tracts that a class 3 student should be able to master. "The low hanging fruit has been picked. But now the serious and more difficult and less visible changes are needed." That is, basic literacy has improved greatly, but the unfinished agenda is huge.[18]

Nand Kishore Singh, Member of Parliament from Kumar's party, has this to say about a free-bicycle scheme to encourage school-going: "The bicycle project that the Chief Minister introduced, to give every girl student a bicycle to be able to commute to the school, has led to greater girl child enrollment and girl child retention in the state's schools. Later on, the scheme was extended to include boys also who were in need of help." A study subsequently (following the World Bank's field studies) revealed that 97.2 per cent of the money the students received had resulted in the actual purchase of the bicycle. Supplying uniforms to all schools with a particular colour and giving them the money to buy uniforms also helped. The result of all these measures is that the dropout ratio has declined dramatically. On primary health, Amartya Sen had noted, "the improvements the state made in immunisation, child nutrition and all other characteristics inherent in the Millennium Development Goals (MDGs)."[19] However, this success story faces some challenges, too. The first challenge is, can the growth rate of 12 per cent be maintained for the next 20 years? Because even at this rate of growth, it will take Bihar another two decades to catch up with national averages in per capita income, consumption of electricity, number of higher education centres, etc."[20]

How Bihar Tamed Maoists

The boom in GDP and revival of government services had a major impact in Maoist areas of Bihar, which were typically the most backward ones with the least infrastructure. The mass jailing of gangsters led, unwittingly but surely, to the debilitation and fragmentation of the Ranbir Sena, the upper-caste militia, many of whose leaders went to jail. Semi-feudal rural rule at gunpoint became more difficult. Meanwhile Kumar began strengthening the *panchayat* (local government system), which Lalu Yadav had kept ineffective. Kumar saw the empowerment of *panchayats* as a means to combat the power of upper castes (who till then had dominated all elections and indeed all village life) and to give, for the first time, some local-level power to the lower castes and to women. The central law on *panchayati raj* called for one-third of seats to be reserved for women, but Kumar increased this to 50 per cent. The backward castes constituted a majority of the population, and so got elected in droves at the local level. To be sure, local powers and budgets of *panchayats* were very limited. Yet having backward castes and women in positions of any power at all constituted a social revolution in rural Bihar. For centuries, the upper castes had been able to use police complicity and gun power to ignore all laws and rule as feudal lords. The position of women was pathetic in such a semi-feudal society—many were not even allowed to go out of the house or get educated. But once *panchayat* reservations came in, the old feudal 'glass ceilings' for lower castes and women were broken. They ruled in villages that had throughout history been dominated by upper-caste males. This change in the social status of the lower castes and women improved their ability to become entrepreneurial and deal commercially with the upper castes without fear.

This new social revolution converted some (though by no means all) once-rebellious villagers under Maoist influence into a class of aspirers. Maoists once claimed to be the only avenue of hope for the victims of rural feudalism. Nitish Kumar was now able to provide a rival avenue of hope, through social change and economic development. Many villagers who earlier were with the Maoists now became police informers against the Maoists. This helped the police to clear out some Maoist pockets. Maoism in Bihar is by no means dead, but has been tamed.[21]

Table 2.5

Maoism in Bihar

	2001-2005	2006-2010
Violent incidents	1,309	514
Armed encounters	141	115
Civilians killed	760	214
Security forces killed	75	102
Maoists killed	76	70
Maoists arrested	1437	2250
Arms recovered	771	701
Explosives recovered	168 kg	80,771 kg
Land mines recovered	19	431
Cash recovered (₹)	70,820	5.66 million

Source: Bihar police records, 2013.

Table 2.5 compares the last five years of the Yadav era (2001-2005) with the first five years of Kumar (2006-2010). It shows that the number of violent incidents fell from 1,309 to 514, civilian deaths from 760 to 214 and armed encounters from 141 to 115. The number of security forces killed rose from 75 to 102, of Maoists killed fell from 76 to 70, but of Maoists arrested shot up from 1,437 to 2,250. Arms recovered changed only a bit from 771 to 701, but explosives recovered shot up from 168 kg to 80,771 kg, landmines/can bombs recovered improved from 19 to 431, and levy money recovered rose from ₹ 70,820 ($1171.33) to ₹ 5.66 million ($94,333.33).[22]

This represents substantial but not spectacular success. Maoism is in retreat, but is far from vanquished. The important lesson from Bihar is that massive use of force, the favoured approach in some other states, is not necessary and may be counter-productive. Kumar has sought to focus on economic development rather than raids on Maoist camps, and has achieved more success in taming Maoism than other badly affected states like Chhattisgarh and Jharkhand.

The Fiscal Boom and Central Transfers

All Bihar politicians have long complained of 'step-motherly treatment' by New Delhi, and say they have never been given a fair share of Central funds from New Delhi. It is indeed true that Bihar has among the lowest rates of per capita government spending. But New Delhi cannot arbitrarily decide how much to give which state. It has discretion over the allocation of what are called Centrally Sponsored Schemes (CSSs), and these go disproportionately to New Delhi's favourites. But the vast majority of New Delhi's revenues are distributed on the basis of periodic reports of a constitutionally mandated Finance Commission. This decides periodically what share of central tax revenues should go to each state, taking into account various demographic, economic and social indicators, and meeting the needs of states that are especially poor or backward. A separate Gadgil formula decides how the annual plan funds (which come mainly from Central government borrowings) should be distributed among the states, again taking into account factors like population, income levels and other indicators. Nitish Kumar and some economists have argued that these formulae are defective and do not provide enough for the most backward states. But other economists worry that rewarding backwardness and lack of local revenue will provide a perverse incentive to state governments to perpetuate backwardness and fail to raise local tax revenue.

Plan spending, financed mainly by central transfers, has risen 15-fold in Bihar in the eight years since the end of Lalu Yadav's rule. This is not consistent with Kumar's complaint of 'step-motherly' treatment by New Delhi. Rather, it looks as though the state has recovered from self-inflicted wounds arising from the decision of voters to repeatedly vote Yadav to office for 15 years.

Plan spending is mainly on basic infrastructure—roads and bridges, dams and canals, power generation and distribution, education and health. In many countries, the government spends too much, and the *EFSI* would view that as lack of economic freedom. But if the state fails to provide even basic infrastructure, by itself or through partnerships with the private sector, this makes it impossible for private enterprise to flourish, and this lack of public goods militates against economic freedom. Although per capita plan spending in Bihar is almost the lowest among states, this has to be blamed substantially on the state's own politicians, of whom Yadav is only one example. State politicians have historically failed to raise local tax revenue, failed to fulfil conditions for getting funds from CSSs and have failed to provide matching local funds that would enable them to tap central plan allocations. Through most of its history, Bihar has failed to spend as much as its annual plan called for. The shortfalls became truly massive under Lalu Yadav. In 2004-05, Yadav's last year in power, Bihar's plan spending was only ₹ 2,000 crore ($333.3 million). By 2012-13, under Nitish Kumar, it had skyrocketed to almost ₹ 30,000 crore ($5000 million). Yet per capita Plan spending remains the lowest among all states, and is roughly half the national average. This shows how far behind the state had been left in the Lalu Yadav era.[23] The recent fiscal bonanza owed much to the boom in all-India GDP growth, which helped raise central tax revenue at the rate of 25-30 per cent per year, a shower of wealth that was shared with the states under the Finance Commission formula. But fast growth within Bihar also raised the state's own revenue at the rate of almost 30-40 per cent per year.[24]

Although government spending has risen fast in Bihar, GDP has grown even faster. Hence, the state's economic freedom score in relation to 'size of government' has improved from 0.38 in our 2005 report to 0.52 in this report. Its ranking among states has improved from 16th to 14th position on this count. Bigger government spending has not become 'big government' in relation to the size of the economy. This is consistent with the state's improvement in overall economic freedom.

Policy changes in New Delhi have helped Bihar unwittingly. When the United Progressive Alliance (UPA) came to power in New Delhi in 2004-2013, it decided to focus on rural infrastructure through a series of schemes collectively called Bharat Nirman. These included stepped up schemes for rural roads, rural electrification, rural health, urban development and agricultural development. This proved a major blessing for backward states like Bihar. Besides, two major arterial national highways that were launched in the year 2000—the East-West highway (from Assam to Rajasthan) and the Golden Quadrilateral (linking the four major metropolitan cities of Delhi, Mumbai, Chennai and Kolkata)—were completed during Kumar's tenure. Both these passed through Bihar and provided top-class connectivity with neighbouring states at New Delhi's expense. Over and above this came the telecom revolution that swept across India in the late 1990s and provided cheap cell phone calls (just two cents per minute) even in remote rural areas without electricity. Telecom towers ran on diesel, and cell phones themselves could be charged using automotive batteries. So, the cell phone revolution spread even to the most backward areas lacking electricity (like most of Bihar). Infrastructure arrived in the state with a big bang.

This fiscal bonanza enabled Kumar to provide unprecedented funds for his many top priorities. These included his spree of building roads and bridges; filling up vacancies in government services across all sectors, but especially in the police, health and education; and creating a new specialised police cadre to take on the Maoists, hiring ex-army soldiers and training them in counter-insurgency techniques.

The Construction Boom

In the Lalu Yadav era, road construction shrank to tiny proportions. This reflected the government's cash crunch, plus Yadav's belief that roads did not win elections and benefited mainly upper caste car-owners. In the five years from 2001-02 to 2005-06, a total of only 294.39 km of roads were constructed. The nadir was reached in 2005-06 when a pathetic 10.85 km were built/improved (see Table 2.6).

Table 2.6

Completed Road Length in Bihar (km)

2001-02	101.54
2002-03	91.00
2003-04	23.00
2004-05	68.00
2005-06	10.85
Sub-Total	**294.39**
2006-07	983.00
2007-08	1,913.00
2008-09	3,106.26
2009-10	3,473.88
2010-11	2,890.36
2011-12	2,028.84
2012-13	1,428.64
2013-14	1,179.19
Sub-Total	**17,003.17**

Source: Road Construction Department, Government of Bihar, Patna.

Nitish Kumar came with a clear vision of giving top priority to roads and bridges. He knew that, because of the lack of electricity, large scale investment in industry was not possible. But construction and road building required little electricity, and so these sectors could go full steam ahead. He began to utilise the central funds that Yadav had rejected contemptuously, and road construction grew in leaps and bounds— starting with 983 km in 2006-07, rising rapidly to a peak of 3,473 km in 2009-10, before slowing down. In the eight years from 2006-07 to 2012-13, no less than 17,003 km of roads were constructed. This transformed communications in the state. Villages got linked to towns and cities, and commerce boomed.

In Bihar, rivers can be several kilometers wide in the monsoon. So, it is not enough to build roads: bridge building is equally important. Private contractors in Bihar in the Lalu Yadav era were largely part of the mafia, and therefore not reliable builders of infrastructure. Kumar chose a government officer, Pratay Amrit, to turn around the moribund government corporation in charge of bridge building (Bihar Rajya Pul Nirman Nigam; BRPNN). BRPNN was bankrupt and demoralised when Amrit took over. But, blessed with backing from the Chief Minister and ample funds, "Amrit led BRPNN from the brink of bankruptcy and mainframe obscurity back to the forefront of the construction business... The BRPNN, which had completed just 314 bridges in the previous 30 years, successfully executed 336 bridges in just three years."[25]

Private home construction, suppressed by the fear of the mafia in the Yadav era, also skyrocketed. The combination of concentrated state and private spending on construction meant that this sector grew at an astonishing 47 per cent per year for the first five years of Kumar's rule. This was a major driver of the Bihar economic miracle.

The Electricity Crisis

Bihar has by far the lowest per capita consumption (122 kWh) of power among Indian states, less than one-tenth that of Gujarat, Chhattisgarh or Himachal Pradesh (see Table 2.7). No less than 40 per cent of all the state's power is consumed in Patna, the state capital, leaving very little for the rest of the state.[26] Only 3.1 million households out of 18.9 million have electric connections—a mere one-sixth of the total. The national average is much higher at 67.3 per cent.

Lack of power is typically a huge impediment to industrialisation. But industries in Bihar (many small, many in food processing) took off with the economic boom in the last decade, using diesel gensets to generate power. This was expensive power, costing up to ₹ 17 per kWh, against ₹ 4-5 per kWh for grid power. This was viable only for industries in which power was not an important input. Such industries included beer breweries; major breweries have been set up by Cobra Beer and Molson-Coors. Food processing was the most common industry, drawing on the state's substantial agricultural production. But for broader industrialisation, Bihar will have to increase its power generation hugely.[27]

Transmission losses (which include theft of electricity) are a whopping 45 per cent of power generated. No wonder the state electricity board loses money heavily. Theft is often aided by corrupt officials, and the rot runs deep. The majority of villages are not even connected to the state grid.

A striking feature of Bihar is that 98 per cent of its electricity is imported from other states, mainly Jharkhand, a consequence of the state's partition in 2000. After doing nothing to augment power capacity for almost a decade, Bihar has made a start with the 1,980 MW thermal station at Nabinagar in a joint venture with the National Thermal Power Corporation (NTPC), and this will more than double the state's supply. The first unit of 660 MW should be ready by the end of 2013. Another unit of 3,300 MW of capacity is coming up at Barh, doubling state

Table 2.7

State-wise Per Capita Electricity Consumption, 2009-10

States/UTs	*Per Capita Consumption of Electricity (kWh)*
Haryana	1222.21
Himachal Pradesh	1379.99
Jammu & Kashmir	952.02
Punjab	1526.86
Rajasthan	736.20
Uttar Pradesh	348.37
Uttarakhand	1112.29
Gujarat	1615.24
Madhya Pradesh	602.07
Chhattisgarh	1546.94
Maharashtra	1028.22
Andhra Pradesh	966.99
Karnataka	903.24
Kerala	525.25
Tamil Nadu	1131.58
Lakshadweep	
Bihar	122.11
Jharkhand	880.43
Odisha	874.26
West Bengal	550.16
Assam	204.80
Total (All India)	778.71

Source: Press release, Ministry of Power, August 12, 2011.

capacity yet again. Two power purchasing agreements have been signed with private vendors for a total of 1,010 MW, but progress on these is not certain. The new capacities coming up will transform the ability of the state to industrialise and to spread rural electrification.[28]

Bihar's Economic Freedom Indicators have Improved Significantly

Bihar has grown fast and its governance indicators have improved in the last decade. Yet the improvement is not dramatic and looks grossly insufficient. Bihar remains last among the 20 states that this report assesses every year for economic freedom. The state scores exceptionally badly in legal structure and security (see Table 2.8).

Our report looks at three areas of economic freedom. Area 1 relates to the size of government and efficiency. In this regard, Bihar's score has improved from 0.38 in 2005 to 0.52 in 2013, a significant improvement. Its ranking among states has also improved from 16th to 14th position. The top state in this regard, Gujarat, improved its score from 0.56 to 0.69, an increase of 0.13, which is actually less than Bihar's increase of 0.14. Madhya Pradesh, another backward state, suffered marginal erosion in its score from 0.39 to 0.38. So, in this particular area, Bihar did pretty well. Its overall position may be low, but it certainly registered improvement.

Area 3 relates to regulation of business and labour. Here Bihar has improved its score from 0.26 in 2005 to 0.30 in 2013. But its rank among states slipped from 15th to 16th position, meaning other states improved faster than Bihar. Gujarat's score in Area 3 skyrocketed from 0.47 to 0.87, and its rank remained 1st. Madhya Pradesh's score actually deteriorated, from 0.46 to 0.39. However, its rank is still a respectable 8th, well above Bihar's 15th. In sum, in regard to regulation of business and labour, Bihar under Kumar has improved somewhat, but not impressively.

Where has Bihar done really badly? Surprisingly, it is in Area 2, relating to legal structure and security. In 2005, Bihar was by far the worst in the country in this area, with a pathetic score of 0.12. Astonishingly, our data show no improvement whatsoever in 2013—the state remains last with

Table 2.8

Selected States: Economic Freedom Scores for Area 1 (Size of Govt), Area 2 (Legal Structure and Security) and Area 3 (Regulation of Labour and Business)

	Area 1, 2005	*Area 1, 2013*	*Area 2, 2005*	*Area 2, 2013*	*Area 3,2005*	*Area 3,2013*
Bihar score (rank)	0.38 (16)	0.52 (14)	0.12 (20)	0.12 (20)	0.26 (16)	0.30 (15)
Gujarat score (rank)	0.56 (2)	0.69 (2)	0.35 (12)	0.39 (7)	0.47 (1)	0.87 (1)
Madhya Pradesh score (rank)	0.39 (14)	0.38 (20)	0.63 (2)	0.62 (1)	0.46 (3)	0.39 (8)

Source: *EFSI 2013*, main report.

an unchanged score of 0.12. Indeed, Madhya Pradesh, another backward state that historically has also suffered from dacoits (criminal gangs) in its Chambal Valley, has done fabulously well compared with Bihar. Madhya Pradesh's score was a high at 0.63 in 2005 and is only marginally lower at 0.62 in 2013. It currently comes first among all states in this regard. If a backward, dacoit-infested state like Madhya Pradesh can produce such good scores, why has Bihar lagged far behind in last position? Bihar Chief Minister Kumar's main claim to political and economic success has been his success in jailing mafia dons and gangster-politicians, improving security and thus improving the investment climate. Why does this not show up at all in our measures of legal structure and security?

Let us take a more detailed look at the different elements that go into Area 2. These are: (a) ratio of property recovered to property stolen; (b) inverse of judicial vacancies to judicial posts; (c) inverse of economic offences to total offences; (d) ratio of police investigations completed by year-end; (e) ratio of court cases completed by year-end; and (f) inverse of proportion of violent crime to total crime during the year.

The data is given in Table 2.9. Note that in some cases, the data gives the inverse of a ratio and in other cases the ratio itself. This is because, for ease of review and assessment, we want to always show higher scores as being an improvement. Obviously a higher proportion of stolen property recovered is an improvement. But a higher proportion of violent crime is not an improvement, and so in that element of security we measure the inverse.

Table 2.9

EFSI Scores on Elements of Legal Structure and Security

	Bihar		*All India*	
	2005	2013	2005	2013
Property recovered to property stolen	0.15	0.16	0.26	0.21
Inverse of judicial vacancies/posts	5.77	4.18	6.06	6.52
Inverse of economic/total offences	29.3	24.3	27.3	21.8
Share of police investigations completed	0.62	0.66	0.78	0.74
Share of court cases completed	0.108	0.089	0.150	0.140
Inverse of violent crime to total crime	3.8	5.2	8.73	9.12

Source: EFSI 2013, main report.

The data shows that in regard to recovering stolen property, Bihar has hardly improved at all between 2005 and 2013, with its score edging up from 0.15 to 0.16. At this level, it is some distance from the national average of 0.21. Besides, what the table does not show is that the national average was as high as 0.31 in 2011, driving home again Bihar's deficiencies. While top gangsters may have been jailed in Bihar, more mundane police tasks like detecting crime and recovering property have not improved.

Data on judicial vacancies are discouraging. Bihar's score has declined from 5.77 to 4.18, even as the national average has improved from 6.06 to 6.52. Nitish Kumar has not focused enough on filling judicial vacancies. He has surely been right in paying the most attention to getting the police-judicial system to put the worst mafia dons in jail. Yet, this does not excuse his neglect of mass justice for more humdrum crimes faced by the population.

Again, the ratio of economic cases to total cases has fallen. This means the share of criminal cases has actually risen. This does not necessarily reflect a worsening crime situation. In Lalu Yadav's time, the police simply did not record crimes reported by the public, and the Chief Minister acquiesced. By contrast, Kumar has told police stations to record all complaints. While compliance with this directive is limited, the rising share of crimes reflects more accurate reporting, rather than a worsening situation. It is worth noting that the all-India situation also shows a deteriorating trend. Indeed, Bihar's ratios in both 2005 and 2013 were better than the national average. Does this mean Bihar had much less crime? No, it means Bihar has always recorded far fewer crimes.

The proportion of police investigations completed in the same year has improved in Bihar from 0.62 in 2005 to 0.66 in 2013. The all-India average is significantly better, at 0.78 in 2005 and 0.74 in 2013.

The proportion of court cases completed within the same year shows Bihar in a dismal light. The proportion used to be a low at 0.108 in 2005 and has worsened to 0.089 in 2013. While the courts may have quickly jailed many top gangsters, they remain pathetically tardy in other cases. This in part reflects the high number of unfilled judicial posts. The national average has gone from 0.15 in 2005 to 0.14 in 2013, which may not look like a very good proportion of case completions, but it is well above Bihar's rate.

Finally, the share of violent crime in total crime is falling. This is true of Bihar and of the whole country. However, Bihar's rate continues to be almost double the national average. Things are getting better but remain terrible by national standards.

Crime and Punishment: A Comprehensive Look at Bihar

Why are the police in India so notorious for refusing to record crimes, especially petty or non-violent crimes? In part, this reflects an effort by the police to hide their own inadequacy. In part, it reflects the police practice of refusing to register cases unless the complainant pays a bribe. In some states like Bihar, it also reflects unwritten understandings to do nothing in the case of complaints against gangs known to have important political connections.

The legal structure and security measures considered by our report (Area 2) look at only a few selected crime indicators. We need a much broader look to capture the full essence of the changes that Nitish Kumar has brought about in the state. This is shown in Table 2.10.

Table 2.10

Bihar Crime Statistics, 2001-2012

	2001	2004	2012
Murder	3,619	3,861	3,198
Dacoity	1,293	1,297	556
Robbery	2,175	2,909	1,381
Burglary	3,036	3,191	3,629
Theft	9,489	11,518	16,292
Kidnapping	1,689	2,566	4,211
Kidnapping+ransom	385	411	57
Rape	746	1,063	934
Bank dacoity	22	30	11
All crimes	95,942	115,216	147,633

Source: Bihar Police website: *http://biharpolice.bih.nic.in/*

The overall picture shown by Table 2.10 may dismay the casual observer. Total cognisable crimes rose from 95,942 in 2001 to 147,633 in 2012. The naïve may think this shows that crime has worsened under Kumar. In fact, it shows that reportage of crime has improved. Actual crime has probably fallen: that is strongly suggested by a more detailed examination of the data.

The police find it extremely difficult to suppress murder reports, and so murders can be assumed to be pretty accurately reported throughout the period shown in the table, from 2001 to 2012. The murder rate went up from 3,619 in 2001 to a peak of 3,861 in 2004 (under Yadav) and has come down in the Kumar era to 3,198 in 2012. The improvement is significant, but not exactly spectacular. The fact is that many murders relate to quarrels within families or villages, and such killings are not affected by a change of chief ministers. More significant is the reduction in other types of murder—by the mafia, private militia, and Maoists. Unfortunately the website of the Bihar Police gives no such breakdown of murders.

A good indicator of changing security conditions relates to dacoity, which means armed attack by a gang of five or more persons. Its incidence has fallen from 1,293 in 2001 to 556 in 2013, a big improvement. Bank dacoity is down from 22 to 11 cases. Robbery (by less than five persons) is down substantially from 2,175 in 2001 to 1,381 in 2012. Remember that improved reportage means that the actual fall in all three cases must be far greater than the reported fall.

However, reported burglaries are up from 3,036 to 3,629, and reported theft is up from 9,489 cases to 16,292. This almost certainly reflects better reportage.

Reported rapes have increased from 746 to 934. This is one crime that the police are particularly reluctant to record, and one that victims are reluctant to report too (more so in Yadav's time, when some of the perpetrators were seen to have political protection). The rise in numbers of rapes probably reflects better reportage, rather than worsening crime. Women claim they feel much safer in the Kumar era and can be seen roaming in Patna's markets till late evening. By contrast, markets virtually shut down by 6 pm in the Yadav era.

Kidnapping was a big issue in Yadav's time. Readers may be surprised to learn from Table 2.10 that total kidnappings have more than doubled, from 1,689 in 2001 to 4,211 in 2013. How does this square with improved security under Kumar? Answer is: in Bihar (as also in many other Indian states), when a young couple elopes, the girl's parents typically report it to the police as kidnapping by the young man concerned. The sharply increased numbers probably represent more accurate reportage of elopements, not an epidemic of elopements or kidnappings.

The really serious kidnappings are those accompanied by ransom demands. These are typically aimed at the richest families, and in the Yadav era, these struck terror among investors, who stopped investing. The number of kidnappings with ransom demands rose from 385 to a peak of 411 in 2004 and is now down to just 57 in 2012. This is a big improvement. Three things stand out. First, it is not necessary for kidnappings to go into thousands to have a terrible impact on the investment climate: a few hundred are enough if the gangsters are seen to have political protection. Second, data on actual kidnappings for ransom are misleadingly small, since they cloak the far higher number of demands for protection money which people chose to pay to avoid kidnapping. There are no data on this, but the problem was huge in the Yadav era. Third, despite much improvement under Kumar, the menace has clearly not ended.

The bottom line is that the quality of governance remains poor in Bihar, and the crime and punishment scene leaves much to be desired. There is indeed much improvement, but it is from terrible to bad. This is to a fair extent reflected in our own EFSI indicators, which show some improvement in Bihar but nothing spectacular.

Conclusion

Our economic freedom index is correlated with growth of state GDP, but not very strongly. The main reason is that Bihar is an exception that weakens the all-India correlation. This state has consistently been rock bottom among states in its overall score for economic freedom, yet it has been among the fastest growing states between 2005 and 2013.

In the preceding section, we took a closer look at the different elements of the economic freedom index for Bihar. We compared that with the performance of the best state, Gujarat. We also compared Bihar's performance with that of Madhya Pradesh, which is another of the historically poor and backward states. The comparison showed that Bihar had very weak economic freedom indicators in relation to not just prosperous Gujarat but even poor Madhya Pradesh. Yet Bihar's growth has been almost as fast as Gujarat's, and markedly faster than that of Madhya Pradesh.

Clearly, our EFSI indicators are unable to capture some key elements of economic reality and dynamism in Bihar. Bare crime data do not reveal the improvement: improved accuracy of reportage of crimes can produce very misleading data that cloak reality. The real increase in security is far greater than the bare data suggest. When anarchy and gangster rule end and a semblance of security returns, this can spark a huge improvement in investment and consumer purchases, producing rapid economic growth. This effect was evident in Peru after the quashing of the Shining Path guerillas, and was also evident in the northern districts of Andhra Pradesh after the quelling of Maoism there. This effect is especially notable when the restoration of security coincides with economic reforms that improve economic freedom, something that happened in both Peru and India. Fast growth created by the end of anarchy may not be sustained after some time in Bihar. But in Kumar's nine years rule, it has sufficed to facilitate double-digit GDP growth. Our economic freedom indicators have not been able to capture the quality of this security breakthrough.

Second, under Kumar, annual plan investment in the state has shot up 15-fold. This has been used fairly well (despite continuing corruption and waste) in basic infrastructure, education and health. It has been absolutely key in helping spark Bihar's fast growth, by greatly improved productivity. Note that even after such a big increase, per capita indicators of all sorts (including plan investment) in Bihar remain among the lowest in all states. The huge rise in the state's plan spending reflected three factors. The first was much higher utilisation of funds that were earlier available but not availed of by Lalu Yadav, taking advantage of a low base effect. The second was the economic boom in India between 2004 and 2011, which hugely increased central government revenues and the share of these going to the states. The third was the bonanza in Bihar's own revenue: double-digit growth produced annual growth of 30-40 per cent in state revenue.

However, the state's GDP has risen even faster than government spending, so the state's freedom score in respect of 'size of government' has improved substantially, from 0.38 in our 2005 report to 0.52 in this report.

This suggests that spending so far has, by and large, been productive, stimulating enterprise in the overall economy. The danger remains that if government spending continues rising at this pace, it could go into wasteful and inefficient projects and programmes.

The factors aiding Bihar's dizzy growth are slowing down. The low base of the Yadav era has gone. India's GDP growth, which was as high as 9.2 per cent in 2010-11, fell to 6.5 per cent in 2011-12, 5.0 per cent in 2012-13, and may fall again this year. This has slowed central revenues and will slow the growth of Bihar's revenues too. This may be partially offset by a change in formula for plan investment in different states: Bihar is likely to be a gainer from the re-defined formula for backward states. Yet, the recent tearaway pace of growth of transfers from New Delhi will slow down.

India suffers from structural problems that have slowed GDP growth in ways that will not easily be reversed. New laws have ushered in new rules and regulations relating to the environment, tribal areas, forests, mines and land acquisition, and these have led to long delays and a slump in productivity. This will inevitably affect all states. Bihar believes it may be less affected than other states: being one of the least globalised states, it has the least to lose from India's recent decline. But without stronger economic reforms in both New Delhi and Patna, Bihar's days of double-digit growth may be over.

Endnotes

1. Basu, Kaushik (2013). "The Bihar Economy: An Overview and Some Field Notes", N.K. Singh and Nicholas Stern (eds.), *The New Bihar*. Penguin.
2. Aiyar, Swaminathan S. Anklesaria (2013). "Lessons in Good Governance from Bimaru States", in N.K. Singh and Nicholas Stern (eds.), *The New Bihar*. Penguin and Aiyar, Swaminathan S. Anklesaria (2013). "Lessons in Good Governance from Former Bimaru States: Bihar, Odisha and Chhattisgarh", *The Economic Times*, March 18.
3. Mukherji, Arnab and Anjan Mukherji (2013). "Sushasan: Governance and the New Bihar", in N.K. Singh and Nicholas Stern (eds.), *The New Bihar*. Penguin.
4. Ibid.
5. Aiyar, Swaminathan S. Anklesaria (2013). "Can Growth Tame Maoism?", *The Economic Times*, April 1.
6. Matthew, Santosh and Mick Moore (2011). "State Incapacity by Design: Understanding the Bihar Story", *Working paper* 366. Institute of Development Studies.
7. Ibid.
8. Mukherji and Mukherji *op. cit.* no. 3.
9. Conversation of Nitish Kumar with the author in March 2013.
10. Aiyar, Swaminathan S. Anklesaria (2013). "Lessons in Good Governance from Bimaru States", in N.K. Singh and Nicholas Stern (eds.), *The New Bihar*. Penguin.
11. Basu *op. cit.* no. 1.
12. Mukherji and Mukherji *op. cit.* no. 3.
13. Srivastava, Amitabh (2013). "Nitish's Most Favoured Dons", *India Today*, July 1.
14. Mukherji and Mukherji *op. cit.* no. 3.

15. Aiyar *op. cit.* no. 5.

16. Rangaraju, Baldeva, James Tooly and Pauline Dixon (2012). *The Private School Revolution in Bihar: Findings from a Survey in Patna Urban*. Academic Foundation.

17. Ibid.

18. Bannerj, Rukmini (2013). "Elementary Education: Learning the Hard Way", in N.K. Singh and Nicholas Stern (eds.), *The New Bihar*. Penguin.

19. Sen, Amartya (2013). "Bihar: Past, Present and Future", in N.K. Singh and Nicholas Stern (eds.), *The New Bihar*. Penguin.

20. Singh, N.K. (2013). "The Making of the Bihar Growth Story", in N.K. Singh and Nicholas Stern (eds.), *The New Bihar*. Penguin.

21. Aiyar *op. cit.* no. 5.

22. Ibid.

23. Press Trust of India (2009). "Bihar has the Lowest Per Capita Plan Spend", *The Economic Times*, November 18.

24. Mundle, Sudipto (2013). "Raising and Managing Resources for a Stronger Bihar", in N.K. Singh and Nicholas Stern (eds.), *The New Bihar*. Penguin.

25. Srivastava, Amitabh (2012). "Prataya Amrit: The Man who Built Bihar's Road to Success", *India Today*, March 30.

26. Parekh, Deepak (2013). "The Power Sector: Times for a Big Leap", in N.K. Singh and Nicholas Stern (eds.), *The New Bihar*. Penguin.

27. Ibid.

28. Ibid.

3

The Centre and the States

Excessive Centralisation Hampers Economic Freedom

Bibek Debroy

The economic freedom scores and inter-state rankings in this report facilitate the tracking of a state's performance over time. India is a federal country, and this is set out in the Indian Constitution. However, one doesn't often appreciate how centralised India is, and the extent to which the centre impinges on the freedom of the states.

The widespread use of the phrase centre-state relations is itself symptomatic. It is an expression that is very widely used but reflects a patronising mindset, suggestive of a centre and a periphery. The bedrock of all Indian policy should be the Constitution, which always refers to a union government, not 'the centre.' Yet the Commission that was set up to study relationship between the union and the states, as a successor to the Sarkaria Commission, with a report submitted in March 2010, was also called a Commission on Centre-State Relations.[1] The point that India is excessively centralised, especially in comparison with China, has often been made.[2] In part, the reason was historical and colonial and this was reinforced by developments after Independence. "Looking back and as is well known, in the first three decades after the independence centralisation of powers had been accentuated due to various factors such as the predominance of a single political party at the Centre as well as in the States; adoption of planning as a strategy of national development in which investment decisions determined by the Union, albeit through a consultative process, generally set the priorities for state budgets; the system of industrial licensing and control; and nationalisation of major banks. The trend of judicial pronouncements during this period also tended to follow a similar spirit."[3]

This is in contrast to a considerable amount of cross-country literature on the benefits of decentralisation. One has to be careful in using the word 'decentralisation', because it can be used to mean different things and not all of these have something to do with governance. Within the ambit of decentralised governance, there are many aspects such as political decentralisation, administrative decentralisation, fiscal decentralisation and economic decentralisation. Some arguments in favour of decentralisation are based on efficient provision of public goods and services, and on optimal levels of governance relating to economies and diseconomies of scale in providing these public goods and services. Others are linked to making decision-making participative. However, decentralisation is not only about union-state relations. It is also about decentralisation and devolution within a state, and about empowering local governments, the third tier of governance.

The Problem of Excessive Centralisation

There are some issues that the Commission on Centre-State Relations called Constitutional Governance and the Management of Centre-State Relations.[4] The Constitution has one list of subjects that are under the jurisdiction of the union government, another list of topics under the jurisdiction of the states and yet another list of concurrent subjects involving the joint jurisdiction of the union and the states. This raises several issues.

First, it has often been the case that even when subjects are in the Concurrent List of the Seventh Schedule, the union has not effectively consulted states on key issues, such as the drafting of legislation before introduction in Parliament.

Second, the Inter-State Council provided for in the Constitution has not functioned efficiently.

Third, there is a strong case for moving non-tax-related residuary powers from the Union List to the Concurrent List. As of now, all residuary powers vest with the union.

Fourth, when a bill has been passed by a state legislature and sent to the state governor, and the governor in turn refers it to the President, there are no time limits prescribed. The system is completely open-ended, and this empowers the President—who acts on the advice of the union government—to put off approval or disapproval for as long as the union government feels like it.

Fifth, New Delhi has often misused its authority in appointing and removing governors of states, who have no executive powers but can recommend the dismissal of state governments and holding of fresh elections. This provides the ruling party in New Delhi with a lever of control over the states: it can appoint party hacks who will do its bidding to the extent possible.

Sixth, discretionary powers of the governor, including invoking Article 356 (dismissing the state government), have been misused in the past. These should be curbed.[5]

Seventh, the states participate in the Inter-State Council, the National Integration Council and the National Development Council. But other key decision-making bodies such as the Planning Commission and Finance Commission function as extensions of the Union Government, and have no representation from states. They should.

Eighth, the Rajya Sabha (the upper house of Parliament) is elected by state legislatures and is meant to reflect the interests of states. But in 2003, the law was changed to allow persons from anywhere in India to be elected to the Rajya Sabha from any state.[6] This contravenes a basic principle of federalism: the representatives of the state should be local persons.

Ninth, the all-India services are elite cadres that provide the top bureaucratic and technocratic staff of the states as well as the union. This reduces the flexibility of the states.

In sum, although India is a federation, it has strong unitary biases. These militate against the spirit of federalism.[7]

Need for Equitable Access to Services

Irrespective of which state they live in, all citizens of the country should have equitable access to private opportunities and to public goods and services. This requires assignment of sources of revenue and provision of public goods to different levels of government. The primary responsibility of the union ought to be the provision of public goods and services that cut across various states and resolve inter-state issues. For example, it can set rules for horizontal competition among states on the supply of various services. However, if one scrutinises the tax and expenditure responsibilities assigned to the union and states in the Seventh Schedule, one detects an imbalance. On an average, states raise 34 per cent of all government revenue and incur 58 per cent of all government expenditure.[8] This 58 per cent expenditure share is also slightly misleading. About 15 per cent of state expenditure is on what are called Centrally Sponsored Schemes (CSSs), given on condition that matching grants come from the states. Consequently, the untied, flexible share in state expenditure is below 58 per cent. State expenditure on CSSs has been increasing over time, so their flexibility in determining expenditure has progressively been declining. The ability of states to finance current expenditure through their own revenue is low and has been declining. This has been compounded by an inability or unwillingness on the part of the states to increase capital receipts (by, for instance, sale of government assets). Hence, states have resorted mainly to borrowing on the capital account to finance not just capital spending but even current expenditure. New Delhi often lectures the states on lack of fiscal prudence. But there is a 'centripetal' bias in the assignment of tax responsibilities: New Delhi decides too many of these.

In one sense, this should not matter. Since 2000, following the 10th Finance Commission's recommendations, all central taxes are treated as a common divisible pool between New Delhi and the states. However, this is a finite kitty, and there are competing claims between states. Standard questions regarding vertical equity (between the union, states and possibly local governments) and horizontal equity (between states) have been examined by all Finance Commissions. The 13th Finance Commission observed, "There is spatial inequality in the fiscal capacity and fiscal needs of different states. The reasons underlying this spatial inequality vary considerably, depending on the state in question. Further, different states are at different stages of the development transformation, so their fiscal needs also vary over time. The Constitution provides general guidance on addressing the needs of the states and the Centre as well as taking account of state-specific needs."[9]

States have different fiscal capacities. But the broader background must also be remembered. For example, as a result of post-1991 reforms, a sector that has grown fast is services, and to a lesser extent is manufacturing. Therefore, states that could best stimulate these sectors have grown faster, and this has been reflected in faster revenue generation. States that could not stimulate these two sectors have suffered in relative terms.

Central Public Sector Enterprises (CPSEs) have been used for decades to develop disadvantaged regions, to try and produce balanced regional economic development. However, this has not worked well. Many such investments were capital-intensive and generated little local employment (as in the Rourkela steel plant in the tribal wilderness of Odisha). Besides, attempts at regional development were foiled for decades because the union government mandated a freight equalisation policy that made raw materials like steel, coal, iron ore and aluminium available at uniform prices throughout the country. The aim was to promote industry everywhere. The aim failed because many commodities were produced in backward states that would normally have become hubs for conversion of commodities into value-added manufactures. But freight equalisation took away this natural advantage and shifted it to states that already had major industrial hubs, good infrastructure and cheap access to international trade through ports. West Bengal and Bihar were among the biggest sufferers of freight equalisation, and they complained that they were getting de-industrialised and losing out to coastal states like Maharashtra, Gujarat and Tamil Nadu. However, the subsequent abolition of freight equalisation in the 1990s did not produce an automatic return of industry to Bihar and West Bengal: the dynamics of change had permanently made the coastal states much more attractive to business.

Bank nationalisation in 1969 was meant to help spread banking throughout the country. While this did indeed happen, the credit/deposit ratios turned out to be low for many poor, backward states and high in the advanced states. This means that the savings of backward states were diverted to investment in richer states with high credit-deposit ratios.

The unit cost of providing public services varies from state to state. States with difficult mountainous terrain and inaccessible areas bear higher costs for service provision. The citizens of such states suffer from horizontal inequity. They can migrate to other states, of course, but that is not the aim of policy.

The more advanced states are in a position to tap private sources of funds, including capital markets. This option is not easily available to relatively backward states, which tend to have a history of weak governance and poor policy. Thus, financial markets tend to widen development differences between states. However, states with improved policies and governance can narrow the differences.

Article 293 of the Constitution does allow states to borrow. But this is circumscribed by Article 293(3).[10] This means that, without the permission of the union, states cannot borrow from the market, as long as they are indebted to the union. It is impossible to think of scenarios where states will not be indebted to the union. Thus, borrowing by the states from the market is controlled by the union. Since 1985, state overdrafts with Reserve Bank of India (RBI) are also controlled by the union. This disadvantages the states greatly.

Many poorer states possess forests and minerals. If forests are to be preserved, then these should be considered a national public good. Environmental issues also crop up in many sorts of global negotiations. The Government of India's standard reaction is that the premium placed on protection of the environment should bear some relationship to a country's level of economic development. Yet, the same logic is not applied when it comes to protecting the environment in a relatively backward state. No special financial provisions are made for states that bear the brunt of the financial burden (and lack of development opportunities) arising from forest conservation, biodiversity conservation and other sorts of conservation. Enormous reserves of coal and iron ore lie in protected forests where mining is banned. This is one reason why India, which has some of the world's largest reserves of iron ore and coal, nevertheless imports both.

Horizontal Equity between States

Once the vertical share of the union and states has been determined, one needs to ensure horizontal equity (fair distribution between different states). Union-state fiscal transfers (sharing tax revenue) take place through the recommendations of periodic Finance Commissions. New Delhi also borrows for capital spending, and this sum is shared with the states via the Planning Commission. This provides New Delhi with discretionary power over what and where to invest, through central investment and CSSs. The Constitution lays down a mechanism for transfers only through the Finance Commission. It does not provide for any other channel to distribute the net proceeds of taxes to states. There is no provision in the Constitution for what are called Plan-transfers. These have been justified under Article 282, but the Constitutional legality of this is questionable.[11] Even if this is constitutionally legal, it cannot have been the spirit of Article 282. In any event, before 1969, such Plan transfers were on the basis of specific schemes. However, with these becoming broad-based and with the Planning Commission increasing in importance, the Finance Commission's transfers are restricted to tax devolution and grants to cover non-Plan current expenditure, with grants-in-aid covered by Article 275 of the Constitution. This excludes Plan spending (on public investment). The distinction between Plan and non-Plan spending is artificial and questionable. It prevents one from taking an integrated view of spending, even for the limited purpose of transfers to states. For instance, the building of a school is Plan investment but salaries to teachers are non-Plan spending, and putting the two into separate compartments hurts the interests of integrated education.

Besides, after the economic reforms of 1991, the role of government planning itself is questionable. From the 4th to 9th Finance Commissions (that is, 1964-1990), Plan expenditure and grants for capital expenditure have been excluded from the purview of the Finance Commission, whose terms of reference have been progressively diluted.[12] One therefore needs to abolish the Plan *versus* non-Plan distinction and drastically reduce transfers through the Planning Commission. This will restore the Constitutional primacy of the Finance Commission.

Let us first look at the transfers, which are based on formulae. The formulae used by the Finance Commission vary from one Finance Commission to another, but are generally based on population, income, area, tax effort and fiscal discipline. There is a conceptual problem with this. Grants are meant to address the backwardness of a state, and backward states are clearly entitled to larger grants. But having already been compensated in this manner, why should they be compensated a second time through the use of backwardness indicators (population, distance, area) in the formulae for sharing tax between states?

The intent of Article 275 of the Constitution was to provide grants-in-aid to backward states. But if Finance Commissions adopt a gap-filling exercise to compensate backward states for their poor service provision, this can provide a perverse incentive to states to keep their services in bad shape. Hence, indicators like tax effort and fiscal discipline are taken into consideration by Finance Commissions. States are divided into general category states and special category states. General category states get 10 per cent of their devolved funds as grants and the rest as loans, but the share of grants is 90 per cent for the special category states.

The special category states are Arunachal Pradesh, Assam, Himachal Pradesh, Jammu & Kashmir, Manipur, Meghalaya, Mizoram, Nagaland, Sikkim, Tripura and Uttarakhand. These are not necessarily the most economically deprived. There are low income states within the general category too. Special category status is not cast in stone and there have been progressive additions to the list. The Planning Commission lists hilly and difficult terrain, low population density and/or sizeable share of tribal population, strategic location along borders with neighbouring countries, economic and infrastructural backwardness and non-viable nature of state finances as criteria for determining special category status. But there is non-transparency and arbitrariness in its application. Being a border state is apparently one of the most important criteria, and it's far from obvious why this should be the case.

Grants-in-aid should aim at reducing gaps in physical and social infrastructure, making special provisions for tribal populations and funding internal security problems (Maoism, secessionism) that a state might face.

The current indicators of backwardness (population, income, area) are all imperfect. As regards population, the formula sticks with the 1971 state population figure. This aims to avoid penalising states that promoted family planning and rewarding states that did not. It may be desirable to have low rates of population growth, but the concept has been greatly eroded by the fact that what used to be called 'population explosion' is now called 'demographic dividend.' In any event, why should tax devolution be used as an instrument for rewarding family planning? Public services must be provided to all, whether a state has a high or low birth rate.

Finance Commissions use variations of income and area in deciding how revenues should be shared between states. In fact neither income levels nor area are good criteria: they tell us very little about the quality or effectiveness of public services, for which they are getting a share of central revenues. It would be better for Finance Commissions to stick to output indicators such as actual service provision.

Finance Commissions compute tax effort and fiscal discipline in different states. This is a difficult exercise. In attempting this, the Finance Commissions make no attempt to estimate the overall resource position of a state. Instead, they start with base-year figures and make normative projections into the future. In no case have the projections of Finance Commissions matched actual outcomes, especially for backward states.[13] This has unwittingly but seriously punished backward states. [14]

Reduce Flows through the Planning Commission

We must reduce fund flows through the Planning Commission. Such transfers have both discretionary and non-discretionary elements. For non-discretionary transfers, the Planning Commission used the Gadgil formula from 1969 onward and a modified Gadgil-Mukherjee formula from 1991 onward. The current formula provides that 30 per cent of available funds are reserved for the special category states. Many others, notably Bihar, have argued that if the economic backwardness is a relevant criterion for transfers, many other backward states should also be in the special category.

Typically, the special category states are given funds on the basis of plan projects. But the general category states obtain funds, out of the balance, on the basis of population (60 per cent), per capita state domestic product (SDP) (25 per cent), performance (7.5 per cent) and special problems of these states. Of these, special problems of these states only amount for a 7.5 per cent weight. Unlike in the case of special category states, the devolution of central funds to general category states is not based on planned investments or the resources already with states. This is not logical. The difference in the grant/loan ratio to the two types of states is not based on any good logic either.

Next, consider discretionary transfers by the Planning Commission through central sector schemes (investment of New Delhi) and CSSs. CSSs are limited. Most transfers occur through CSSs that require matching contributions from general category states. "Thus, these schemes have grown both in volume and number over the years, in spite of the states' objection to the proliferation of such schemes and the decision of the National Development Council (the country's apex planning body, which includes all Chief Ministers of states) in 1970. The Planning Commission's own view on CSSs, at least in the course of the Tenth Plan, was the following."[15] "It would be better to do a fewer things well rather than messing up with a larger number of activities. ...One of the ways to reduce the mismatch between the lofty intentions of the GoI and its poor implementation capability is by re-examining the whole concept of Centrally Sponsored Schemes, and by radically limiting its number and improving its flexibility. The share of the CSSs in the Plan budget of the Central Ministries has now increased to 70 per cent against 30 per cent in the early 1980s. This massive increase has however not been matched by improved monitoring, and effective control over diversion of plan funds for salaries and other non-plan expenditure. Therefore, the number needs to be curtailed drastically from more than 200 today to just about 20 to 40 so that systems for their monitoring can be developed. No Ministry should be allowed to run more than 3 or 4 CSSs, and the outlay for each scheme should not be less than ₹ 100 crores a year. At present, less than 20 per cent of the CSSs have an outlay of more than ₹ 100 crores a year. Weeding out smaller schemes will therefore reduce the total number of CSSs from 210 to about 40."[16] The Commission on Centre-State relations also recommended, "The number of Centrally Sponsored Schemes (CSS) should be kept to the minimum...Once a programme has passed the pilot stage and has been accepted as desirable for implementation on a larger scale, it should appropriately form part of the State Plan. The Central assistance towards CSS should be kept to a minimum in relation to the Central assistance for the State Plans."[17] No such dramatic pruning has yet been done.

Other than efficiency, delivery and focus, there are other problems with CSSs too. They encroach on items that are on the State List. In 1996, at a conference of Chief Ministers, it was agreed that all CSSs that impinge on the State List should be transferred to states. But that has not happened. Conditions for CSS transfers are imposed on states, often in areas that are the legislative domain of states. CSS transfers are often made to autonomous bodies, bypassing the states. Some CSSs require the creation of a fresh and new bureaucratic system of delivery. In any event, CSSs amount to a unilateral decision by the union to divert resources that would otherwise have been available to states. Therefore, CSSs should be pruned, and more untied funds should be made available to states. These need not be completely untied: there can be overall guidelines and some indication of the sector for which the funds can be used. Subject to these, states need to have far greater flexibility in spending. If, for instance, the aim is to reduce infant mortality, the best way to accomplish it will not be same in Jharkhand as in Kerala. For that matter, the priority of infant mortality reduction will vary from one district to another within the same state. The design of CSSs is extremely centralised and is done in Delhi, without any bearing on what a state really needs. With such central templates, it is understandable that implementation leaves a lot to be desired.

This report focuses on economic freedom in the states. But the union comes in the way of ensuring such economic freedom and imposes many constraints. True economic freedom requires far more decentralisation and devolution of powers and revenues to the states.

Endnotes

1. *Report of the Commission on Centre-State Relations*, Government of India, March 2010.
2. See, for example, Bardhan, Pranab (2010). *Awakening Giants, Feet of Clay, Assessing the Economic Rise of China and India*. Oxford University Press.
3. *Report of the Commission on Centre-State Relations, http://interstatecouncil.nic.in/volume1.pdf*
4. This was the title of the second volume of the report, *http://interstatecouncil.nic.in/volume2.pdf*
5. There are also issues on Article 355, which has implications for the deployment of central forces.
6. Through an amendment to the Representation of the People Act.
7. See, Jha, L.K. (1991). *Towards a Decentralized Polity*, Raja Chelliah Memorial Lecture, The Fiscal Foundation and Guhan, S. (1993). "Centre and States in the Reform Process," in Robert Cassen and Vijay Joshi (eds.), *India: The Future of Economic Reform*. Oxford University Press.
8. Govinda, M. Rao and Nirvikar Singh (2005). *Political Economy of Federalism in India*, Oxford University Press. The data in this book are dated, since they are from the late-1990s. However, though the numbers will change if updated, the thrust of the argument will not.
9. *Report of the Thirteenth Finance Commission, 2010-2015*, December 2009.
10. "A State may not without the consent of the Government of India raise any loan if there is still outstanding any part of a loan which has been made to the State by the Government of India or by its predecessor Government, or in respect of which a guarantee has been given by the Government of India or by its predecessor Government."
11. "The Union or a State may make any grants for any public purpose, notwithstanding that the purpose is not one with respect to which Parliament or the Legislature of the State, as the case may be, may make laws." Constitution of India.
12. That pressure from the Planning Commission was responsible for this dilution is evident from the account given about non-acceptance of the recommendations of the Third Finance Commission. See, Chanda, A. (1965). *Federalism in India* George Allen and Unwin.
13. This shows up clearly in the survey done in Srivastava, D.K. and C. Bhujanga Rao (2009). Review of Trends in Fiscal Transfers in India. Madras School of Economics. July.
14. See, Govinda, M. Rao (2009). "Reform of Intergovernmental Fiscal Arrangements for Balanced Regional Development in a Globalizing Environment," and Govinda, M. Rao and Subrata Mandal (2009). "Resource Endowment, Fiscal Flows, and Regional Equity in Indian Federalism", in M. Govinda Rao and Anwar Shah (eds.), *States' Fiscal Management and Regional Equity, An Overview*. Oxford University Press.

15. *http://planningcommission.nic.in/reports/articles/ncsxna/ncsax2a.htm*. More accurately, this was the view articulated by N.C. Saxena, but it was also a general view.
16. *Report of the Commission on Centre-State Relations*, Government of India, March 2010.
17. *http://interstatecouncil.nic.in/volume3.pdf. http://interstatecouncil.nic.in/volume7.pdf* is also relevant.

Appendices

APPENDIX I

Variables and Methodology

Description of Variables used for Economic Freedom of the States of India 2013

Normalised Variables	*Variables*	*Units*	*Source*
Area 1: Size of Government: Expenditures, taxes and enterprises			
GSDP/Revenue expenditure	GSDP at Current Prices	₹ crore	CSO and estimates
	Revenue expenditure	₹ crore	RBI, State Budgets
% of GSDP accounted for by public administration	% of GSDP accounted for by public administration	%	CSO
Total organised employment/ employment	Total employment in organised sector	in '000	Directorate General of Government Employment & Training, Ministry of Labour
	Total employment in government and quasi-government institutions	in '000	Directorate General of Employment & Training, Ministry of Labour
GSDP constant prices/ State taxes on income	GSDP (2004-05 prices)	₹ lakh	CSO and estimates
	State revenues from income tax	₹ lakh	State Finances, RBI
GSDP constant prices/ State taxes on property and capital transactions	GSDP (2004-05 prices)	₹ lakh	CSO and estimates
	State revenues from taxes on property and capital transactions	₹ lakh	State Finances, RBI
GSDP constant prices/ Taxes on commodities and services	GSDP (2004-05 prices)	₹ lakh	CSO and estimates
	State revenues from taxes on commodities and services	₹ lakh	State Finances, RBI
Inverse of Stamp Duty Rate	Stamp Duty Rate	%	*www.indiaproperties.com*
Area 2: Legal structure and security of property rights			
Total value of property recovered/Value of property reported stolen	Total value of property recovered	₹ lakh	National Crime Records Bureau
	Total value of property reported stolen	₹ lakh	
Total number of posts in judiciary/Vacant posts	Total judiciary posts sanctioned in district/subordinate courts	Number	Government of India (GoI)
	Vacant posts of judicial officers in district/subordinate courts	Number	
Total cases/Economic offences	Total incidence of crimes under Indian Penal Code (IPC)	Number	National Crime Records Bureau
	Economic offences (criminal breach of trust, cheating and counterfeiting)	Number	
Cases completed by police/ Total cases registered with police	Cases where investigation completed by police	Number	National Crime Records Bureau
	Total cases registered for investigation by police	Number	

contd...

...contd...

Normalised Variables	*Variables*	*Units*	*Source*
Trials completed by courts/ Total cases for trial by courts	Total number of trials completed by courts	Number	National Crime Records Bureau
	Total number of cases awaiting or undergoing trial by courts	Number	
Total cases/Violent crimes	Total incidence of crimes under IPC	Number	National Crime Records Bureau
	Cases of murder, attempt to murder, culpable homicide not amounting to murder, rape, kidnapping and abduction, preparation and assembly for dacoity, robbery, riots, arson and dowry deaths	Number	
Area 3: Regulation of labour and business			
Yearly average of daily wages for harvesting (males)/ Minimum notified wages	Yearly average of daily wages for harvesting (males)	₹	Labour Bureau, Ministry of Labour, GoI
	Minimum notified wages	₹ per day	Wage Cell, Ministry of Labour, GoI
Yearly average of daily wages for harvesting (females)/Minimum notified wages	Yearly average of daily wages for harvesting (females)	₹	Labour Bureau, Ministry of Labour, GoI
	Minimum notified wages	₹ per day	Wage Cell, Ministry of Labour, GoI
Total number of industrial workers/Man days lost in strikes and lockouts	Total number of industrial workers	Number	Annual Survey of Industries Data, Central Statistical Organisation
	Man-days lost in strikes and lockouts	Number	Industrial Disputes in India, 2001, Ministry of Labour, GoI
Minimum licence fee for traders	Minimum licence fee for traders	₹ per annum	Ministry of Agriculture, GoI
Actual Industrial Entrepreneurs Memorandums (IEMs)/ Value of proposed IEMs	Actual value of IEMs that were implemented	₹ crore	Secretariat for Industrial Assistance, GoI
	Total value of proposed IEMs	₹ crore	Secretariat for Industrial Assistance, GoI
Met peak demand/ Peak demand	Met peak demand for electricity	MW	Ministry of Power, GoI
	Peak demand for electricity	MW	
Total cases registered for corruption/Cases pending investigation	Total cases for investigation under prevention of corruption and related acts	Number	National Crime Records Bureau (NCRB)
	Cases pending investigation from previous year	Number	

contd...

...contd...

Normalised Variables	*Variables*	*Units*	*Source*
Total cases registered for corruption/Persons arrested for corruption	Total cases for investigation under prevention of corruption and related acts	Number	NCRB
	Persons arrested under prevention of corruption and related acts	Number	

APPENDIX II

Detailed Methodology

The Economic Freedom Index (EFI) has been calculated for 20 states of India. Ideally, all 35 states and union territories should have been included; however, data unavailability prevented this. As a result, only those states and union territories are included for which data were available for most of the variables that are used to construct the index. No imputations were made.

Further, many variables that would have found a suitable place in this index could not be included as data were not available for many states. Eventually 21 variables covering diverse aspects of economic freedom in different areas were utilised to arrive at the composite freedom index. There were a few variables for which data were not available for some of the 20 states. However, since the indicator was essential for the credibility of the index, such indicators were retained.

There are many different ways of constructing a composite index. One way of doing this is to assign subjective weights to different variables. However, in order to ensure objectivity, this ranking refrains from such an exercise. No subjective weights have been used and as a result each variable is considered to be equally important.

The following steps were followed in constructing the index:

1. Identifying the appropriate variables: The variables in the freedom index were chosen to enable a comprehensive view of economic freedom could be obtained while working within the constraints of data availability.

2. Normalising the variables: Indian states vary in geographical area, topography, social and economic milieu. Depending on the variable and what it aspires to measure, each variable has been appropriately 'normalised'.

3. Comparability of data: Since data are collected at the state level, care has to be taken to ensure that the data are defined in the same way for different states and also that they are for the same time point. Further, since the ranking exercise implies that higher values reflect better performance, appropriate ratios have been developed. Often this implied taking an inverse of a particular indicator or subtracting a percentage from 100.

4. Creating an index of each variable: While the composite index gives an overall view of freedom, it may be that while a state performs extremely well in certain indicators, its performance may not be as satisfactory in others. An index of each variable or indicator is

also constructed, so that a ranking of the states is available for a detailed understanding of the situation of freedom. Details of the construction of individual indices are presented below.

5. Creating a composite index for each category: The simple arithmetic mean was used to calculate the category indices.

6. Calculating a composite/overall index: This final step required all three category indices to be aggregated to arrive at a composite indicator of relative economic freedom for 20 states.

The last three steps in constructing the EFI are now explained in detail.

Creating an index of each variable: An index is obtained for each of the 24 ratios as mentioned earlier. The following formula was used to obtain each of the 24 indices:

$$I_{ij} = \frac{S_{ij} - Min(S_{1j}, S_{2j}, \ldots, S_{20j})}{Max(S_{1j}, S_{2j}, \ldots S_{20j}) - Min(S_{1j}, S_{2j}, \ldots, S_{20j})},$$

where S_{ij} represents the value of ratio *j* for state i. The index is constructed for 20 states of India and therefore i ranges from 1 to 20. There are 21 ratios for which the indices have been constructed, j = 1,2,..., 24. I_{ij} is the index value that is derived for state i over ratio *j*. The index value lies between 0 and 1 for each ratio. The state corresponding to index value 0 can be interpreted as having the lowest level of economic freedom and the state with index value of 1 can be said to have the highest level of economic freedom relative to other states.

Note that the maximum and minimum values are the same as those used for earlier years, this ensures that the index values are comparable over time.

Creating a composite index for each category: Arithmetic mean was used to calculate the category index as follows:

$$C_{ik} = \frac{\sum_{j}^{n} I_{ijk}}{n},$$

where C_{ik} is the category index of the ith state for the kth category over *n* indices within the category.

Calculating a composite/overall index: Once all the indices for the 24 ratios were obtained, a composite index was obtained using all these indices. An arithmetic mean of all the indices helped to arrive at the additive index.

The formula used to calculate the composite index is as follows:

$$M_i = \frac{\sum_{k=1}^{N} C_{ik}}{N},$$

where M_i is the additive index value for the ith state over the N category indices of freedom. Here N is 3.

APPENDIX III

Mapping of Variables with Economic Freedom of the World

EFW Categorisation		*Variables at the State Level for India*
Area 1: Size of Government: Expenditures, taxes and enterprises		
a) General government consumption spending as a percentage of total consumption	1.	Government revenue expenditure/Gross State Domestic Product (GSDP)
	2.	Administrative GSDP/Total GSDP
b) Transfers and subsidies as a percentage of GDP	3.	Subsidy on power for domestic consumers/ Population
c) Government enterprises and investment as a percentage of GDP	4.	Govt. employment/Total organised employment
	5.	Percentage of State Level Public Sector Enterprises (SLPSEs) in which disinvestment completed or initiated
d) Top marginal tax rate (and income threshold to which	6.	State taxes on income/GDP it applies)
	7.	State taxes on property and capital transactions/GDP
	8.	Taxes on commodities and services/GSDP
	9.	Stamp duty rate
i. Top marginal tax rate (excluding applicable payroll taxes)		Data not available: Also many different types of state income taxes
ii. Top marginal tax rate (including applicable payroll taxes)		
Area 2: Legal structure and security of property rights		
	10.	Total values of property recovered/ Total value of property reported stolen
	11.	Vacant posts in judiciary as a ratio of total posts sanctioned
a) Judicial independence: The judiciary is independent and not subject to interference by the government or parties in disputes		Not Applicable
b) Impartial court: A trusted legal framework exists for private businesses to challenge the legality of government actions or regulation		
c) Protection of intellectual property		
d) Military interference in the rule of law and the political process		
e) Integrity of the legal system	12.	Cases under economic offences/Total cases
	13.	Per cent cases where trials were completed by courts
	14.	Per cent cases where investigations were completed by police
	15.	Violent crimes
Area 3: Access to sound money		
a) Average annual growth rate of money supply in the last 5 years minus average annual growth of real GDP in the last 10 years		Not Applicable

contd...

...contd...

EFW Categorisation		*Variables at the State Level for India*
b) Standard inflation variability in the last 5 years		Inflation rate calculated on basis of GDP deflator
c) Recent inflation rate		
d) Freedom to own foreign currency bank accounts domestically and abroad		Not Applicable
Area 5: Regulation of credit, labour and business		
a) Credit market regulations		
i. Ownership of banks: Percentage of deposits held in privately owned banks		Financial sector overseen by central government, no state level differences
ii Competition: Domestic banks face competition from foreign banks		
iii Extension of credit: Percentage of credit extended to private sector		
iv Avoidance of interest rate controls and regulations that lead to negative real interest rates		
v Interest rate controls: Interest rate controls on bank deposits and/or loans are freely determined by the market		
b) Labour market regulations		
i. Impact of minimum wage: Minimum wage set by law has little impact on wages because it is too low or not obeyed	16.	Average wage of unskilled workers/ Minimum wages
ii. Hiring and firing practices: Hiring and firing practices of companies are determined by private contract	17.	Man-days lost in strikes and lockouts/ total number of industrial workers
iii. Share of labour force whose wages are set by centralised collective bargaining	18.	Unorganised labour force as a ratio of organised labour force
iv. Unemployment benefits: The unemployment benefits system preserves the incentive to work		Not Applicable
v. Use of conscripts to obtain military personnel		
c) Business regulations		
i. Price controls: Extent to which businesses are free to set their own prices		
ii. Administrative conditions and new businesses: Administrative procedures are an important obstacle to starting a new business	19.	Minimum Licence fee for traders
iii. Time with govt. bureaucracy: Senior management spends a substantial amount of time dealing with government bureaucracy	20.	Implementation rate of Industrial Entrepreneurs Memorandum (IEM denotes the intention to invest, but when there are bureaucratic or other delays, the rate of implementation is lower)
iv. Starting a new business: Starting a new business is generally easy	21.	Power shortage as a percentage of total demand (power shortage exists either due to low investment on the part of the government or due to low levels of private sector generation)
v. Irregular payments: Irregular payments connected with import and export permits, business Licences, exchange controls, tax assessments, police protection or loan applications are very rare.	22.	Cases pending investigation from previous year of cases registered under prevention of corruption and related acts as a share of total cases registered under the same acts
	23.	Persons arrested as a share of total cases being investigated under prevention of corruption and related acts

APPENDIX IV

Data and Results

APPENDIX TABLE IV.1

Area 1—Size of Government: Expenditures, Taxes and Enterprises, 2013

State	*Inverse of Government Revenue Expenditure as a Share of Gross State Domestic Product (GSDP) (2011-12)*	*Inverse of Administrative GSDP as a Ratio of Total GSDP (2011-12)*	*Inverse of Share of Government in Organised Employment (2010-11)*	*Inverse of State Level Taxes on Income as a Ratio of GDP (2010-11)*	*Inverse of Ratio of State Level Taxes on Property and Capital Transactions to State GDP (2010-11)*	*Inverse of State Level Taxes on Commodities and Services to GDP (2010-11)*	*Inverse of Stamp Duty Rate (2010-11)*
Andhra Pradesh	8.61	0.25	1.51	1,378	164	17	0.20
Assam	5.03	0.12	2.10	441	436	21	0.12
Bihar	6.61	0.17	1.07		204	29	0.08
Chhattisgarh	7.00	0.24	1.12	15,367	131	17	0.13
Gujarat	10.36	0.32	2.52	2,608	107	19	0.13
Haryana	10.91	0.40	1.76		133	21	0.08
Himachal Pradesh	4.78	0.17	1.45		461	18	0.13
Jammu & Kashmir	3.44	0.06	1.05		527	19	.
Jharkhand	6.45	0.19	1.27		354	23	0.08
Karnataka	8.49	0.26	2.15	821	124	13	0.10
Kerala	9.42	0.22	1.81	6,955	123	17	0.12
Madhya Pradesh	7.01	0.19	1.17	1,349	110	15	0.13
Maharashtra	11.73	0.20	2.05	740	85	21	0.20
Odisha	7.70	0.24	1.20	1,697	281	22	0.07
Punjab	7.55	0.21	1.69		106	17	0.17
Rajasthan	8.21	0.24	1.33		150	20	0.10
Tamil Nadu	8.76	0.25	1.60		134	15	0.13
Uttar Pradesh	6.39	0.14	1.32	27,038	97	20	0.07
Uttaranchal	8.19	0.15	1.36	9,825	208	24	0.07
West Bengal	8.39	0.19	1.68	1,339	154	33	0.14

APPENDIX TABLE IV.2

Area 2—Legal Structure and Security of Property Rights, 2013

State	Ratio of Value of Property Recovered to the Total Value of Property Stolen (2011)	Inverse of Vacant Posts in the Judiciary to the Total Number of Sanctioned Judicial Posts (2011)	Inverse of Total Number of Cases under Economic Offences to the Total Number of Cases (2011)	Percentage of Cases where Trials were Completed by the Police (2011)	Percentage of Cases where Trials were Completed by the Courts (2011)	Inverse of Violent Crimes as a Ratio of Total Crimes (2011)
Andhra Pradesh	0.52	7.15	17.03	0.76	0.23	14.20
Assam	0.22	3.90	26.96	0.40	0.19	5.84
Bihar	0.16	2.41	24.35	0.66	0.09	5.23
Chhattisgarh	0.39	11.48	46.71	0.89	0.13	10.83
Gujarat	0.20	2.11	41.21	0.86	0.07	17.09
Haryana	0.42	4.07	23.44	0.76	0.24	9.30
Himachal Pradesh	0.30	8.80	28.28	0.73	0.08	11.72
Jammu & Kashmir	0.50	17.08	28.96	0.76	0.11	6.50
Jharkhand	0.19	6.09	26.05	0.59	0.25	4.60
Karnataka	0.36	5.88	21.52	0.76	0.21	8.46
Kerala	0.02	10.40	31.01	0.83	0.19	11.71
Madhya Pradesh	0.36	8.70	89.38	0.94	0.19	13.96
Maharashtra	0.12	9.27	18.08	0.64	0.07	8.57
Odisha	0.32	5.92	37.12	0.72	0.09	6.17
Punjab	0.74	4.38	8.92	0.63	0.19	9.32
Rajasthan	0.61	5.39	9.05	0.96	0.13	15.48
Tamil Nadu	0.54	9.10	43.99	0.62	0.28	14.21
Uttar Pradesh	0.40	7.80	14.01	0.88	0.23	5.92
Uttaranchal	0.35	2.11	13.29	0.83	0.10	5.63
West Bengal	0.21	6.43	25.38	0.61	0.04	7.03

APPENDIX TABLE IV.3

Area 3—Regulation of Labour and Business, 2013

States	*Ratio of Average Wage of Unskilled Workers (Males) to Minimum Wages* (2010-11)	*Ratio of Average Wage of Unskilled Workers (Females) to Minimum Wages* (2010-11)	*Inverse of Man-days Lost in Strikes and Lockouts/Total Number of Industrial Workers* (2010-11)	*Inverse of Minimum Licence Fee for Traders* (2002)	*Implementation Rate of Industrial Entrepreneurs Memorandum (IEM)* (2010-11)	*Inverse of Power Shortage as a Percentage of Total Demand* (2011-12)	*Inverse of Pendency Rate of Cases Registered under Corruption and Related Acts* (2012)
Andhra Pradesh	1.74	1.26	2.66	0.04	0.040	1.00	1.77
Assam	1.42	1.30	1.40	0.10	0.063	0.96	1.13
Bihar	1.14	1.06	0.87	.	0.004	1.00	1.49
Chhattisgarh	1.84	1.63	5.14	0.00	0.003	0.96	1.46
Gujarat	1.53	1.44	14.23	0.20	0.085	1.00	2.09
Haryana	1.37	1.35	2.20	0.05	0.184	0.90	1.57
Himachal Pradesh	2.20		9.83	.	0.062	0.79	1.46
Jammu & Kashmir	2.69	2.69	.	.	0.123	0.75	1.36
Jharkhand	1.14	1.06	36.60	.	0.007	0.92	1.25
Karnataka	1.57	1.04	8.06	0.01	0.019	0.87	1.67
Kerala	4.47	3.58	0.89	.	0.068	0.91	1.20
Madhya Pradesh	1.84	1.63	2.69	0.00	0.036	0.94	1.94
Maharashtra	1.52	1.06	1.22	0.33	0.052	0.93	1.68
Odisha	1.70	1.51	.	.	0.001	0.93	1.56
Punjab	1.30		3.94	.	0.068	0.76	1.31
Rajasthan	1.62	1.51	0.91	0.01	0.100	0.95	1.53
Tamil Nadu	3.75	2.69	3.12	.	0.040	0.88	1.70
Uttar Pradesh	2.68	2.30	1.14	0.00	0.103	0.86	1.59
Uttaranchal	0.70	0.64	9.68	.	0.106	0.95	1.00
West Bengal	1.37	1.34	0.04	0.01	0.051	0.99	1.67